YOU
PROBABLY
SHOULDN'T
WRITE THAT

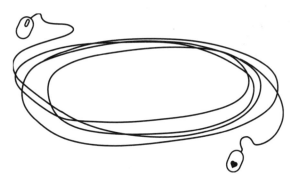

178

YOU PROBABLY SHOULDN'T WRITE THAT

TIPS AND TRICKS FOR CREATING AN ONLINE DATING PROFILE THAT DOESN'T SUCK

LISA HOEHN

RUNNING PRESS
PHILADELPHIA · LONDON

*Books published by Running Press are available at special discounts for
bulk purchases in the United States by corporations, institutions, and other
organizations. For more information, please contact the Special Markets
Department at the Perseus Books Group, 2300 Chestnut Street, Suite 200,
Philadelphia, PA 19103, or call (800) 810-4145, ext. 5000, or e-mail special.
markets@perseusbooks.com.*

ISBN 978-0-7624-5886-8
Library of Congress Control Number: 2015954108

E-book ISBN 978-0-7624-5904-9

9   8   7   6   5   4   3   2   1
Digit on the right indicates the number of this printing

Cover design by Frances J. Soo Ping Chow
Interior design by Mike Rogalski
Edited by Sophia Muthuraj
Typography: Brandon Text

Running Press Book Publishers
2300 Chestnut Street
Philadelphia, PA 19103–4371

Visit us on the web!
www.runningpress.com

To my family, a constant reminder that hope is
one of the most important things in life—
and that you should never let it go.

And to Liam Hemsworth, because I know that
if you ever read my online dating profile,
we'd be together forever.

CONTENTS

YOU'RE A **LOVER,**
NOT A **WRITER**

What You're Going to Get Out of This Book— and Why the Hell I'm the One Writing It

I'm a serial online dater—which means I've sent and received thousands of messages, corresponded with hundreds upon hundreds of men, and been on (without exaggeration) at least one-hundred first dates. I've fallen in love, fallen in like, and fallen flat on my face. (Literally. Didn't get a second date out of that one.)

But I wasn't always so cavalier about online dating. In fact, when I first moved to New York City fresh out of college, I had landed my dream job working in editorial at a big women's magazine and was working seventy-plus-hour weeks, seeing hardly anything besides my cubicle walls and crappy apartment, and had resigned myself to being in a relationship with work. It took a solid year before the ever-increasing pangs of loneliness—and the realization that the only men who had asked me out were my office doorman and the chubby bartender with bad teeth downstairs—forced me to consider turning to the Web. Even then, I was too chicken shit to follow through.

That's when my younger sister visited. Sick of hearing me complain about the lonely life of a single woman in the big city (cue sad violin), one evening she fed me a bottle of wine, went to the OkCupid home page, and told me that it was time.

"But I don't have any good photos of myself!" I told her. "What would I even say in my profile?" Undaunted by my half-hearted, drunken protests, she set to work—and an hour (and another bottle of red) later, I sat on my bed staring at my profile.

I couldn't tell you what that first profile said or even what photos she chose. I can tell you that my then-teenaged sister was far from a writer, and what she created didn't feel like me. I was so intimidated by the idea of writing my own profile that I honestly didn't care. The page was done . . . and I figured that should be enough to get me out there.

At first it was. My inbox filled up fast (blame it on being a young woman in a big city). And so the dates began.

There was the guy who spent our entire evening talking about hypothetical animal battles (you know, mastodon versus panther, alligator versus elephant, etc.). There was the taxidermist, the clown (who *brought his red nose to our date* and even *put it on*), and the guy who claimed to be getting his PhD in philosophy but who actually worked at a pizza shop, just, you know, musing. There was even the man who "accidentally" spent way-y-y too much time in the women's restroom before realizing his mistake and strolling leisurely over to the men's.

And then there was Jeff. We made plans at the last minute, and he suggested meeting at a wine bar in his neighborhood. I arrived first and was immediately impressed by the venue: small and candlelit, yet cute and unpretentious. When Jeff walked in, I was even more impressed. He looked just like his pictures, but was somehow handsomer in person. Tall, dark hair, a short, well-kept beard, dressed like a man who cared about the clothes he put on . . . and as he said hello, his voice nearly made me melt into my shoes. Finally, I thought, a date that won't end with the urge to sprint out the door.

We ordered a carafe of wine to share, and conversation flowed effortlessly. We talked about our mutual love for improv comedy, and he made me laugh. As the wine dwindled I assumed we were ready for another round, but when the waiter arrived, Jeff spoke up: "We'll take the check."

Turning to me, he let out a weak sniffle. "I could really use some nose spray, so I should get going," he explained in a newly nasal voice. "But I live just around the corner, and I have a bottle of wine in my apartment, if you'd care to join me."

It all became clear. "Needing nose spray" was his move. The charming man with whom I thought I had a connection had one thing in mind: sex. Heaven forbid he entice me to his place with a killer music collection, a cute animal, or the promise of a funny sitcom—a fine mist of nasal decongestant, so he thought, should do the trick.

I did sprint out of the bar that night, determined to call it quits with online dating. But as I arrived home, it hit me: my problem wasn't the population of men on OkCupid (well, at least not entirely); my problem was my profile. Not only had it been created by a tipsy teen, but it was also short and sloppy—and didn't accurately represent who I was or what I was looking for in a match or relationship. It was no wonder the guys who responded positively to it weren't whom I wanted, either.

So I logged back into OkCupid, this time unafraid and determined to write something that felt like *me*. I spent hours over the next couple weeks writing, rewriting, and tweaking the text and photos, running every change by both my male and female roommates to get feedback. And then one day, I was done—I finally had a profile that I was proud of.

That's when everything started to get better. Suddenly the messages I was receiving changed—instead of being formulaic (as, I only then realized, they had been before my overhaul), they made references to specific details in my profile. They asked questions that I wanted to answer. Refreshingly, the men on the other end seemed interested in getting to know me as opposed to talking to everything with a vagina and a face.

Which is when it dawned on me that I wasn't the only one who had been going on miserable dates . . . and therefore, I wasn't the only one who needed help with my virtual dating presence. Everyone did. Which is when it also dawned on me that between my experience with online dating and my background as a writer and journalist, I had the chops—and wanted to be the one—to provide that help.

So, combining my skills and expertise, I started a business, ProfilePolish. com, dedicated to helping people improve their online dating profiles. Now I help beleaguered online daters around the globe polish their profiles, gain confidence, and generally up their online dating game every single day.

At least in theory, online dating shouldn't suck. After all, you're crafting the text and curating the photos that could be your future husband's or wife's first impression of you—and what should make you feel more empowered than finally abandoning the bar scene, the YMCA singles dodgeball leagues, and the bad setups and instead charging headfirst into the vast virtual dating pool? As it turns out, for a lot of people, almost anything. When I asked one man how confident he felt about his online profile on a scale of 1 to 10, he said this:

-43,312,516,265,110,547,789,549,148,103,813,444,568,421 . . .
continue on nonrepeating for infinity much like pi.

Oof.

A 23-year-old guy, when probed about his profile writing, simply said:
While I know that I'm a decent writer, I feel like I do a horrible job of selling myself. My profile has gone through several iterations, and while I feel like they all describe me (or at least aspects of me), my personality doesn't really shine through.

But that's far from all I've found out about what online daters think. These feelings of nervousness, insecurity, and self-consciousness are everywhere. Here's a tiny smattering of the things that my clients have told me about their profiles.

From a 36-year-old female executive living in a big city:
I really don't like talking about myself. I do love to own a room, but it's weird to write about myself . . . is it too wordy? Am I saying the right things? I just feel like the wrong guys are responding. No one that I am really attracted to or has the same kind of background as me—and then I see cute guys who seem like men whom I would want to talk to, but they view me and don't write . . . and I just sit there wondering what's wrong with me!!

From a 54-year-old man getting back out into the dating world for the first time in decades:
My written profile is boring, long, and normal. There's very little wit and humor, and there's nothing unique. And when I try to be funny, it feels forced. I like profiles that are genuine, confident, and humorous, without being cocky. I tried to write as such, but with no luck!

From an otherwise confident 26-year-old woman:
I have no idea what pictures to put up. Are they attractive enough? I don't think I look good enough to get anyone to click on my profile.

And from a 33-year-old:

> *I'm really a nice guy, but I don't know what I'm doing. I feel like the profile does a rubbish job of selling me. In person I am pretty good at winning people over, but the profile seems like a barrier to meeting people. I try to power through the sections, but re-reading and editing just magnifies my self-doubt.*

But that's not the worst of it. Some people will try anything to pen a profile that works, like this smart, eloquent, 45-year-old woman:

> *I'll tell you something embarrassing. . . . A girlfriend sent me a profile of someone who met [her] husband on a site—and the profile has been circulated around a few friends under the heading of "this one works!" So we used it, changed the details to suit us, but mostly used it as it was. Sadly, it doesn't work.*

But it doesn't have to be this way.

Whether you're a frustrated online dating veteran, are just getting back into the game after a breakup or divorce, or are a total virtual virgin, by the time you get done reading this book, you'll have kissed that self-doubt good-bye—and won't need me to do a thing.

You'll learn about choosing the platform that will give you the best chance at landing your perfect match. I'll help you brainstorm facts and details about your life and identify the most attractive parts from an outsider's perspective. With easy-to-follow directions, you'll be able to come across as both articulate and conversational in your profile, all while staying true to who you really are. Not to mention that I'll teach you everything from what photos will get views to how to start a conversation with someone you're interested in and when to turn that communication into a face-to-face meeting.

Ultimately you'll gain the skills you need to create an online dating profile that will make total strangers want to meet you, date you, and fall in love with you . . . until online dating doesn't suck.

Let me serve as proof. Once I fixed up my online dating profile, everything changed. Not long after my virtual makeover, I received a message from a guy who talked about his favorite hiking spots and asked me about mine. We chatted back and forth and finally picked a night to meet up in the city. Half an hour after our arranged meeting time, I was ready to walk out of the bar—when he walked in. Tall, broad shouldered, and dark haired, looking disheveled enough to know that he had clearly run there from the train; we locked eyes, and I suddenly didn't care about the thirty minutes I had waited.

Andrew apologized profusely—he had been signing the lease for his new apartment and it had taken seemingly forever (which was as good an excuse as any that I could think of)—and we soon moved on to talking about everything from college football to our favorite movies and swapping camping stories. He laughed easily, and I followed suit. Two hours later, he asked if I wanted to step out of the bar quickly because he had a surprise. I was confused, but trusted him enough to cautiously follow. As he pulled a flask out of his jacket pocket, he told me that he had brought a bit of his favorite rare bourbon—all because he had seen my love for the brown water on my profile. Which is precisely when I kissed him.

Things moved quickly between us, and as I shut down my account I knew that finally my profile had done its job—I was blissed out on online love.

WHAT A POLISHED PROFILE CAN DO FOR YOU

Whether you're creating a profile for the first time or are ready to give yours a virtual facelift, this book is for you. Here's what you can expect to accomplish by employing the techniques laid out in the following chapters.

INCREASE YOUR PROFILE VIEWS. Your main photo and your profile preferences can be the difference between getting views and getting ignored. Knowing what to fill in as well as which pic to choose (and how to edit it to make you stand out in the crowd) can grow the number of users who land on your page.

CHANGE THE WAY THAT YOU'RE PERCEIVED. Online daters have two main ways to make assessments of you—the text and your photos. Between the combo, profiles can exude everything from sex to smarts, casual to committed, and sulky to spontaneous. And the conclusions that outsiders draw change both whether or not and the way that they'll interact with you. Give off the right vibe and you'll be more likely to meet the right person.

UP YOUR MESSAGE RESPONSE RATE. After changing the text in my male clients' profiles, message response rates have been known to go from a depressing 2–3 percent to around an above-average 25 percent—and women have reported similar spikes. If that's not proof that what you say matters, I don't know what is.

IMPROVE THE TYPE, QUALITY, AND CONTENT OF MESSAGES THAT YOU RECEIVE. A great profile provides hooks—or conversational ins—that a smart match will latch onto and use as content in a first message. When he or she does, you're more likely to end up talking about topics that are meaningful and will forge connection between you, both online . . . and maybe even off.

BOOST YOUR CONFIDENCE. When you're proud of your online dating profile, it's less daunting to make the first move—and you're more likely to not only feel good about sending messages and get responses, but you're also more likely to receive messages from interested parties. Bonus: When you're confident, it shows and confidence is sexy.

GIVE YOU A REASON TO LOVE ONLINE DATING (AGAIN). A standout profile can land you better matches, better messages, and better dates. And nothing should be more motivating than that.

CHAPTER 1

PICKING YOUR **PLATFORM**

Tinder, eHarmony, FarmersOnly—the Lowdown on Which Apps and Sites Won't Waste Your Time

There are dozens upon dozens of online dating sites and apps out there, and more are being added to the world every day—think Hinge and Happn. This means it can be daunting when you're ready to take the plunge into the world of virtual romance. Which site (or sites) should you sign up for, and which will waste your time? The answer is that it all depends on what you're looking for—and how you want to find it.

The abundance of choices has led many of my clients to make one of three key mistakes. One 54-year-old female client committed the first error: signing up for the wrong sites entirely. She was looking for a committed relationship when she asked me, "I just don't understand why I can't meet anyone on Tinder or OkCupid. All of the matches and messages that I get are from younger men who have (sometimes pretty gross) sexual fantasies about being with an older woman. What am I doing wrong?"

Then there was the 29-year-old who committed the next sin: signing up for every site under the sun. He was on no fewer than five platforms at once and didn't realize that spreading himself so thin was bound to make matching less effective—after all, he had less time and energy to devote to each site and ended up doing a half-assed job with all of them. It's not only harder to keep track of your matches when you do this, but it's also harder to be an engaged enough user to really get to know the intricacies of a platform and use it to its full potential.

And then there was the 33-year-old guy who was so confused by all the sites that he just got . . . well, stuck. "I'm so overwhelmed—I have no idea which site will work for me and which ones will be duds," he lamented.

But as the cliché goes, knowledge is power, and understanding the ins and outs of the major online dating platforms can not only save you time, energy, and money, but ultimately lead you to your perfect match.

Each of the sites discussed below works in a slightly different way to find you the Cheech to your Chong, but on the screen, they're pretty similar. Each features a profile that you, the user, must fill out. These profiles consist not only of a place to upload personal photos of yourself, but also a text box (or text boxes) wherein you're urged to write unique and original copy to help other users get to know the real you and assess whether you might be compatible.

So where should you invest your time and maybe even your money? Here's the lowdown on the world's top sites and apps.

TINDER

Best for ages: 18–35 years old
Cash: Free; paid upgrade to Tinder Plus $9.99/month for users 29 years old and younger; $19.99/month for users 30 and over
Looking for: casual sex, casual and short-term dating—but hey, you never know

The lowdown: Tinder, a smartphone app, hit the scene and exploded in popularity faster than hipsters invaded Brooklyn and San Francisco. Some estimates claim that it now has more than 100 million users—and those users are incredibly engaged. They spend more time on the app than they do scrolling through their newsfeeds, and this makes matching fast and furious.

Tinder is different from other sites in that there is an optional written bio of no more than 500 characters, leaving you mostly with between one and six photos to decide whether you're interested. To start, you must connect to the app via your Facebook account. After you've set your preferences (the age and gender(s) of your matches and the distance you're willing to travel to meet someone), Tinder uses your phone's GPS to find others who are active in your area. It then shows you a prospective match's main photo; his or her first name, age, and written bio if there is one; as well as whether or not you have any friends or liked Facebook pages in common (information taken directly from your Facebook account). Tap on the profile image of your potential match to scroll through his or her other photos, and when you've decided whether or not you're into him or her, you swipe right, indicating that you "like" someone, or swipe left, giving that person a big "nope." If and only if you both swipe right, you and your match are given a chance to chat within the app.

Tinder also allows you to connect your Instagram feed directly to your account, allowing potential matches to browse your dozens of food pics (and of course, cat pics and selfies), and sports a feature called "moments," with which you can share a photo for twenty-four hours with all those you have matched with, to show them what you're doing, thinking, or looking at—much like a romance-inspired Snapchat.

So what's the deal? On its face Tinder is the most superficial of all the sites, which is why it at first garnered a reputation as a hookup haven. Most of its users eschew a written profile entirely or include text about the length of a tweet, leaving photos to tell their stories. The company claims that users analyze these pics for more than just good looks, taking into account everything from choice of clothing to activity to location—but let's be real: the beautiful people of the world end up with tons more matches than those not blessed with a perfectly symmetrical face.

But the app has made online dating into a game like no other site before it. Swiping through matches is often referred to as "playing," and the company reinforces this, using the same language within the app itself. Of course this doesn't come without problems. I know of many men who simply swipe right on every woman who pops up—giving them the option of chatting with anyone and everyone who also swipes right—but with little intention of starting a conversation with the vast majority of their matches. And while this strategy could also be employed by females, in my experience, women aren't nearly as likely to connect with matches whom they probably, well, aren't really interested in connecting with.

What's more, without the presence of an honest-to-goodness profile, conversations can be pretty lame. "Hey," and "What's up" seem to be the most common conversation starters, and given that there's no substance to them, chatting often fizzles quickly. Of course there's always the occasional person who decides to ask an inane question in the hopes that being unique will prompt a response, but "So, do you like avocados?" isn't exactly what I'd call conversational (or social) wizardry.

But Tinder has managed to crack a code that no other dating site had done before it: making online dating fun and extremely easy. There's little stress in creating a profile, and the hours that you spend working your way through potential mates fly by in a sea of exciting new right swipes and empowering "nopes!" If there had been any stigma left in finding romance via the Internet, Tinder did away with it. And probably most important, the app has taken rejection almost entirely out of the picture. You're swiping through at such speed that it's nearly impossible to remember if you swiped right on someone you didn't match with—and even if you do remember, being passed over with a swipe is far easier to shake off than if you had spent time crafting what seemed like the perfect message.

The bottom line: Tinder is fun, easy, and fast—but thanks to its lack of a substantive profile (and therefore lack of information given), it's best used in conjunction with another dating platform.

PLENTY OF FISH

Best for ages: 22–33 years old
Cash: Free, with optional paid upgraded membership: $8.50/month for a 6-month subscription
Looking for: casual sex, casual dating, possible frustration

The lowdown: Plenty of Fish (or POF, as it's known) is the world's second largest dating platform, with around 23 million unique monthly users. After you fill in a range of information about yourself—everything from whether you're a smoker to whether you have a car to where you fall in birth order—the site's matching algorithm uses information that it has gleaned from couples who left the site in a relationship to learn "which combinations of backgrounds, values, physical attributes, and interests form compatible, lasting relationships." This algorithm also sports a few hard and fast rules—for example, it won't pair you with a smoker or someone with children if you've declared either to be a deal-breaker.

The site then presents you with matches it deems appropriate under a "my matches" header (with premium and extremely active members appearing at the top of your list), but also allows you to browse the site freely, using the search feature to find matches who haven't necessarily been cleared or chosen by the algorithm.

Women can send private images to users of their choosing, although this feature has been disabled for men due to "nudity" (aka too many dick pics).

Finally, there are forums that offer you another place to connect with members, whether you're looking for relationship or profile advice, a place to talk to (and maybe meet) other single parents, or just somewhere to chat about topics from cooking to travel.

So what's the deal? Although POF claims to be the world's largest online dating site, it isn't—and though it also claims that its matching algorithm is sound, many users complain that the only thing they have in common with their matches is their area code. What's more, some users say POF's Web site is clunky, ugly, and difficult to use. Its features are often reported to have bugs, and members complain that the site's population is generally less than committed to online dating, with many users who log in infrequently if at all and who rarely return messages—not to mention that this apathy tends to show in their profiles.

Plenty of Fish also still has a hookup site reputation, garnered early on when it sported a feature called "Intimate Encounters" for adults who wanted some no-strings fun, though this service was done away with in 2013 when the founder claimed that he wanted the site to be about "relationships." With this change, new rules were also implemented; for example, you can't message someone more than fourteen years older or younger than you, and users are urged to report lewd photos or sexual first messages. In spite of all this, when you type "Plenty of Fish" into Google, there are plenty of hits that refer to it as a sleazy site for easy fun.

The bottom line: Plenty of Fish makes plenty of assertions about its standards and its matching abilities, but many of its users are unhappy. Its biggest advantages are free membership and sheer volume of users—so if you've exhausted other sites and not found anyone in your area, POF may provide new options. But in all likelihood, you're better off dropping your line in other waters.

OKCUPID

Best for ages: 22–45 years old

Cash: Free, with optional paid A-list membership: $4.95/month for a 6-month subscription

Looking for: Pretty much anything and everything: friends, casual sex, kinky sex, casual dating, relationships, and marriage

The lowdown: OkCupid claims to be the fastest-growing online dating site and uses a special algorithm, invented by a group of Harvard mathematicians, to match users. How? The site provides hundreds of multiple-choice questions for you to answer at your leisure.

The topics range from sex to movie preferences, politics to smoking habits, and everything in between. Each question consists of several parts, which indicate both your own answer to the question and the answer that your ideal match would give.

For example, OkCupid will ask: "Are you either vegetarian or vegan?"

You answer, in multiple-choice format, "Yes" or "No."

Then you tell the OkCupid computer which answer your perfect match would give: "Yes," "No," or "Any of the above" (the last indicating you have no preference).

Finally, you specify how important it is to you that your match answer in your ideal way: "A little," "Somewhat," or "Very."

If you want to explain the reasoning behind your answer or the requirements you have given, there's a text box to make your case. For example, if you answered that you were, in fact, vegetarian or vegan, that your perfect match would also be a vegetarian or vegan, and that this trait is "very" important to you, you could explain in the text box: "I watched Food Inc. and was never the same again."

Your answers to these questions, unless you choose otherwise, are public on the site. More important, they're also used to calculate a "match percentage" with other users. As long as you answer enough of these questions, answer them honestly, and know what you want in a suitor, OkCupid says it can "find someone who claims to fulfill your claimed requirements, exactly." Theoretically, the higher your match percentage is with another user, the better match you would be in person.

From the moment that you're signed in—with or without a completed profile and whether or not you have answered any multiple-choice questions—you're free to roam around the site, checking out other users' profiles, rating them on a one- to five-star scale, and sending them messages to catch their attention.

Feel like giving users a more personal look into your life? Just like on Tinder, you're free to connect your Instagram feed to your profile.

So what's the deal? No matter who or what you're looking for, you can find it on OkCupid. Because the site is free and only requires an e-mail address (and not even a valid one at that), every kind of person has a profile. Granted, this has given the platform a bit of a "looking for something casual" stigma, but don't be fooled—there's a lot more depth to this site.

The key to making OkCupid work for you is a combination of having a killer profile and taking those match questions seriously. While they're in no way perfect, the more you answer, the more the site can tell what you have in common with different people, and the more accurate your match percentage is going to be. Is answering those questions a pain in the ass sometimes? Yes. But people who cast them aside and immediately dive into the infinite profiles are missing out on the feature that sets OkCupid apart from its competitors.

One warning: Of all of the clients I've worked with, there have been very few over the age of forty five who have been happy on this platform—probably because most of their peers have bitten the bullet and turned to a paid platform.

The bottom line: OkCupid is fantastic for its variety and matching algorithm especially when you're young, but if and when you're exclusively seeking something serious, it can be frustrating to have to wade through the wide array of the site's different types of users.

PRO TIPS FOR OKCUPID USERS

- Skip the multiple-choice questions that don't matter to you in the long haul ("Do you enjoy scary movies?" comes to mind) and instead answer questions that you feel strongly about, marking them "very important." If you have deal-breakers, your answers to these multiple-choice questions allow you to voice them without resorting to negativity in your written profile.

- Vary the topics of the questions that you answer. If you're only answering questions about politics, OkCupid will categorize you as being "very political." The same goes for religion and sex. In addition, incorporating a range of topics in your answers will make you a more well-rounded user, and your match percentages will be more accurate.

- When you're viewing a match's profile in a browser, click the tab "The Two of Us" and use the side panel to sort the questions. My favorites to sort by are, "Unacceptable answers," then "Things that are important to him/her." Sorting by unacceptable answers immediately lets you know whether you'll tolerate that person's views—and by sorting what's important to him or her, you'll get a sense of that person's values compared to your own.

- To keep your profile private, access your "general settings" and click the box that says, "Only allow other OkCupid members to visit my profile." This will stop your page from showing up in a Google search.

Best for ages: 27+ years old
Cash: Paid: $20.99/month for a 6-month basic membership; $23.99/month for a 6-month bundle membership
Looking for: dating, relationships, marriage

The lowdown: If you believe that with age comes wisdom, Match.com might be the site for you—founded in 1995, the platform boasts that more than 75 million profiles have been uploaded since its launch. The site works by asking you for information on everything from your height to your stance on issues from politics to religion—and then continues to ask for your preferences for those same characteristics in your ideal match.

From there, you can click on "mutual matches" to view users with whom you pair highly given your (and their) stated preferences, use the "reverse search" tool to view users who are looking to date someone like you, or just click on the search tab and enter any criteria that you're looking for in a match at that moment. You're then free to send messages and "winks" to whomever you please.

But Match.com isn't just a free-for-all. Using an algorithm officially called "Synapse," the site also takes into account its users' perceived preferences and attempts to match you with compatible users. So if a woman's preferences state that she won't date a man who's under six foot two but is constantly checking out guys who are five foot eight Match.com, like a good friend, will infer that height isn't necessarily a deal-breaker. Then, in the form of a "Daily Matches" e-mail, the site will send her previously unseen matches who may be shorter than six foot two even though that goes against what she says she wants. Match.com requires you to rate the matches it sends you to continue receiving these e-mails and continues to tweak your matches based on the preferences you feed it.

Currently, Match.com's user base has marginally more women than men and consists mainly of thirty to forty-nine-year-olds. Not to be outdone, though, users ages fifty and over are currently its fastest-growing demographic.

So what's the deal? In my experience, the vast majority of Match.com's users are looking for something more serious than casual sex or simple friendships—and are often more committed to making real connections in the real world than users on free sites. This may very well be why it's the most popular dating site on the planet and claims to have spawned more than a million babies.

The bottom line: Match.com offers an extremely diverse user base for people of all ages whose goal is often to find a lasting relationship. Its proprietary algorithm forces you to examine your stated preferences—and sometimes pushing you out of your romantic comfort zone can be precisely what you, and your love life, need.

EHARMONY

Best for ages: 35+ years old
Cash: Paid: $29.95/month for a 6-month subscription
Looking for: serious relationships, marriage

The lowdown: eHarmony isn't for the casual dater—this platform wants to help you find your "soul mate," calling itself "the only resource that uses research-based algorithms and data analysis to identify individuals who are compatible with one another." With a 200-plus-item questionnaire that you're required to fill out at the outset, this algorithm uses your answers to calculate compatibility on twenty-nine levels, ranging from levels of agreeableness to degrees of romantic and sexual passion to the importance of spirituality.

This platform differs in one huge way from the other sites that we've talked about so far, though: it doesn't allow you to freely browse profiles. Instead, the site sends you matches that it deems appropriate, justifying this practice by declaring that having too many options will keep you from deciding on one. Once you've received a match, you have two options: delete that person as a match or start "talking." If you choose to start chatting, you again have two options: use eHarmony's "guided communication," wherein you exchange messages via still-anonymous channels that the site provides, or just jump in and send eHarmony mail. During the "guided communication" process, you and your prospective match can answer eHarmony's preselected multiple-choice questions, reveal your "Makes or Breaks" (aka deal-breakers), or just ask one another questions, which differs from direct in-site e-mail only in that it's still anonymous and allows eHarmony to feed you topics (e.g., "Describe some personal habits that are important to you."). Of course, both you and your match can drop out of this communication process at any time.

eHarmony also recently launched a new service dubbed eH+, a personalized matchmaking package that takes a profile out of the equation entirely. But to go this route is anything but cheap—think $5,000 for an annual membership.

So what's the deal? eHarmony throws a lot of science ("research-based algorithm") and statistics (it claims responsibility for up to 4 percent of US marriages) in your face, but both of these claims have been criticized by academic journals. Not all of its users are pleased, either (a client of mine dubbed the site "eAgony"). Some complain that a large number of the site's users are no longer active, but they remain in the database and therefore can be matched with you. Others say that the site matches them with people with whom they have nothing in common—in spite of the algorithm. And still others have gripes about the number of ads that appear on the site in spite of its hefty membership fee.

What's more, eHarmony originally made sense, to me, as a site for older daters. But with Match.com's fifty-plus demographic growing faster than ever, it's not necessary to hop onto a platform that forces you to spend so much time filling out a questionnaire that feels more like a standardized test than a matchmaking tool—and then to compose answers to prompts such as "the most influential person in my life has been . . ." that feel more like a college-admissions essay than a dating profile.

The bottom line: Many members do find success on eHarmony—especially considering that with that steep membership charge often comes a steep commitment to finding a relationship that will last. If that's your end game, if you'd rather have matches delivered to your inbox than weed through them, or if you're intimidated by the idea of jumping straight into e-mail-esque communication, eHarmony might just be music to your ears.

NICHE DATING SITES

CHRISTIANMINGLE.COM, OURTIME.COM, BLACKPEOPLEMEET.COM, JDATE.COM, AND SO MANY MORE
Best for ages: All ages
Cash: Varies
Looking for: Varies

The lowdown: Whether you're looking for someone who practices the same religion as you, has the same occupation, is the same race, has a disability or a certain sexually transmitted infection, is of a particular age, eats the same way you do, has an accent, or even is just tall, there's a dating platform to help you meet your match. While each has its own unique profile and matching system, these sites let their users feel that at least one of their deal-breakers stays intact.

So what's the deal? According to a Pew Research Center study, up to a third of online daters have tried some sort of niche dating platform. Some sites (such as those discussed above) are large enough to garner millions of monthly visitors, but others (such as FarmersOnly.com, SpiritualSingles.com, and JapanCupid.com) still have a relatively small number of users compared to the online dating behemoths. Sometimes this Internet intimacy can make it easier to sort out those you are and aren't attracted to, but at other times it can leave you feeling frustrated that there simply aren't enough people available.

The bottom line: For those with specific wants or needs in a match, niche dating sites provide a more focused group to choose from—which can cut down on the amount of time spent wading through potential suitors who ultimately wouldn't be a good fit.

CHAPTER 2

SIGNING YOUR ASS UP

The Mandatory Stuff Can Make You or Break You— Without These Smart Strategies

The first time I was curious about online dating, my 22-year-old self timidly visited OkCupid. "Enter your e-mail," it told me. Easy! "Enter your gender," it said. Great! "This isn't so bad," I thought, feeling bolstered. "Maybe I can do this after all!"

Then, on to the next page. "Create a username. This will be public" the site beckoned—and "oh shit," I muttered on cue.

The truth was that I hadn't come up with an interesting and imaginative username since I signed up for AIM in the sixth grade (fizzz2, if you must know). And after having spent many years embarrassed by that third z in my fizz, I started with what I knew and cautiously typed "lisa." I was sure it would be taken, but figured that I'd come up with the rest of it after I had put those four letters out there. What I didn't realize was that OkCupid had (and still has) an autofill generator that will help you come up with a unique username.

"Lisa_taco" and "Lisa_tacosaurus" flashed back at me.

Lisa . . . taco. Lisa taco? Lisa taco dinosaur?!? Although it was probably just nerves, something about the thought of being associated with Mexican food (or somehow worse, a prehistoric Mexican food predator) by the virtual dating populous at large really freaked me out—so much that I immediately shut my laptop and called it quits on OkCupid.

The overarching point, dinosaurs be damned, is that I found coming up with a public username so paralyzing that it caused me to delay joining an online dating site for no fewer than 365 days.

Some sites, eHarmony and Tinder to name a couple, are finally rid of the practice of requiring a unique username, opting instead to feature first names only. But for some reason it seems that on other sites, usernames aren't going away. So it makes sense to cover them here and now—before you, like me, lose an entire year of potential dates thanks to a silly computer algorithm.

The bad news. Consider exactly how many people have signed up for online dating profiles at one time or another. Each has effectively taken a perfectly good (and/or terrible) name away from the rest of us. Singles trying to sign up are constantly hit with the "this username is unavailable" notification. There's even a sketch comedy video that tackles this issue head on, featuring a woman who, after attempting a variety of seemingly sane (and even not so sane) options, ended up dubbing herself "RacistPenisFartCannon." Without venturing into the absurd, it sometimes feels like you may as well not call yourself anything at all. But don't get discouraged just yet.

The good news. Your username is not the end all and be all. Yes, coming up with something takes thought and effort, but in the end, there are only two instances when a potential match will really take notice: when you really nail it or you really screw it up. And screwing it up that badly is pretty tough to do.

USERNAMES: BECAUSE YOU HAVE TO CALL YOURSELF SOMETHING

Whether you're looking to make a serious first impression or fly under the username radar, the following strategies will lead you from the worst to the best pseudonym philosophies.

Fair notice: The usernames below come straight from my brain, but I can't guarantee that there's not someone out there who has claimed one of these as his or her own. So MangoManiac (or whoever you are), my apologies in advance.

Blatant sexual references. Need I say more? Cum2Me. BootysGotABooty. SexyNSassy69. Unless your profile is made purely with the intention of finding casual sex (and even if it is), this type of username screams, "I'm gross" and "I have the maturity level of an adolescent," and alienates 98 percent of users. Steer clear. W-a-a-ay clear.

Lots and lots of numbers. It's tempting to pick any username and add 1234 to the end to claim it as your own. Or to add your birth year, birthday, or lucky number. But ultimately these numbers either date you (literally), don't mean anything to the world at large, or don't mean anything at all. They're distracting, they detract from the rest of what you've come up with, and they make you look unoriginal and dull by broadcasting that you're probably the thousandth person to dub themselves "YogaGirl."

Your last name. Especially when others have scooped up seemingly every name that you can think of, it's all too easy to rely on your given name to fill in the blanks. And if you've been blessed with a last name that has always afforded you a cool nickname growing up (or even still does), you figure, why not use it online, too? But the first letter of your first name followed by your last name isn't only boring, it can be dangerous: Do you really want to be immediately Google-able by everyone swimming in the digital dating ocean?

Outright bragging. Whether it's in reference to your degrees, your accomplishments, or even the number of times you exercise per week, no one likes a braggart—especially in something as obvious as a username. SevenPhDs. MakesLotsofMoney. BigGunsGuy. GucciGirl. Arrogance and superficiality will come across loud and clear and will doom you to online loneliness.

Anything related to tacos or -sauruses. If you're on OkCupid, you clearly just used the bot to create your username, and everyone knows it. Lame.

A series of random letters. Eifxkndk is not a username. It is a mess—and makes you look like one too.

MEH

Your first name. It's not the worst offense, but you can do better. Sure, it may be the path of least resistance to eschew imagination and opt for your first name plus some inane words or numbers (I'm looking at you, Mike-loop, A2_Karen, and HilmJared), but this strategy is simply . . . safe, predictable, and very, well, meh.

Combining interests. Putting two interests or an adjective and an interest together can be descriptive and tell a match something about what you're into, but this tactic is employed so often that it's almost become cliché. And good luck finding one that's not taken. TheRunningTraveler. MuseumMadrigal. TattooedTrails. HikingHippie. CatLovingCook.

Describing your looks. Your height, your body type, your hair color, your gender, and adjectives that describe said looks are easy fallbacks that land you squarely in the middle of the pack. ACuteRedhead. CurvyGirl. TooTallSaul. CurlsAndPearls. BuffDude4You. HeresMyBeard.

OH YEAH

Puns and wordplay. Who doesn't love a good pun? And clever wordplay establishes that you're possessed of a quick wit and sense of humor. Plus, this tactic often presents an entryway into conversation. MatzoBallinSoup (for someone who's Jewish . . . or, you know, anyone who likes matzo ball soup). 2EdsRBetterThan1 (for a guy named Ed). BachToTheFuture (for a musician). Mathletica (for a left-brained fitness fanatic). LastManCamping (for an avid backpacker). NomDeBloom (for a gardener). HotSocket (for a handyman).

Pop culture references. Do you have a celebrity doppelgänger? Are you obsessed with a character on a popular TV show? Do certain music lyrics really speak to you? Draw inspiration from the media that you love to make yourself stand out. Sure, your reference may go straight over some people's heads, but you'll not only catch the attention of the matches out there who do get it, but also give them a shared interest to message you about, to boot. LilSebastianLover. NotBradleyCooper. NoSleepSinceBrooklyn. FondlesMySweaters.

The association game. The idea here is to connect two phrases with a common word in the middle. Try to choose two things that you're interested in—that way, you can show a match what you're into, prove that you have a brain, and stand out from the masses. MatchBookofMormon. TinaTurnerClassicMovies. CaptainPlanetarium. HungryHungryHippocampus. PodCastAway. SpinTheBottleRocket.

The absurd. You may not feel comfortable going there, and not everyone will probably agree that this is a good idea. But going way out with your username—whether it's silly or just nonsensical—is bound to catch someone's eye. The key is to maintain humor and lightheartedness (offending people won't get you anywhere). When someone gets your sense of humor, he or she will feel an immediate connection . . . and want to make one with you. LaceyIsTheLlama. PenguinMurder. BaconBoogers. BirdsWithShoes.

A/S/L AND THEN SOME: DON'T BLANK ON THE BASICS

Now that you've taken care of your completely unique and ultimately awesome username, it's time to move on to what should be the easy part: the multiple choice demographic-type questions and fill-in-the-blank answers.

After all, before you come close to filling out the text on your profile page, dating sites want to know—and display—the basics. But that's a pretty subjective term, and basics don't stop with driver's license info such as your age, sex, and location. Almost all sites go deeper, probing to show prospective matches details like your ethnicity, body type, and astrological sign—and depending on the platform, may even provide a place to display your income, the languages you speak, and your personality type (which can apparently mean anything from Brogrammer to Tree Hugger).

Sites also ask for information about your potential match. Usually that consists of the gender of your match and the age range that you're willing to date within, but it can expand into preferences for everything from height to religion to level of education.

Don't let these prompts throw you for a loop. This is the part of your profile that can and should be the easiest thing you're going to do. And—no matter how much you do or don't like the truth—honesty is always the best policy when it comes to listing this information.

Here's what's usually mandatory:

About You
- Your age
- Your sex
- Your location
- Your relationship status (single, separated, divorced, widowed, seeing someone, etc.)
- What type of relationship you're looking for (friends, short-term dating, long-term dating, casual sex, etc.)

About Your Match
- Gender(s)
- Acceptable age range

   Hint: When you list the acceptable age range of your match, don't go with ages either exclusively younger or exclusively older than your own. Even if you're sure that you want to date either older or younger, blatantly stating age-related deal-breaking parameters for the world to see can make you look close-minded, shallow, and ageist—and will lower your chances with all matches, no matter their age.

Apart from these prompts, on many sites almost anything else asked is optional. And that's the beauty of this section. If you don't feel comfortable answering a certain question, just leave it blank. There's nothing wrong with wanting to keep some personal information private or wanting to disclose certain bits only after you've met someone in the flesh.

What it comes down to is this: don't be shy about listing your information, but if you feel uncomfortable with certain questions, don't answer them.

FUDGING THE FACTS

As I mentioned, I believe wholeheartedly that being honest will yield better results than fussing with the truth. But it's also no secret that some people lie in their profiles—and often right there in the basics. Why do they do it? Usually it's because they think that it will make them either more attractive to prospective matches or more visible on the site itself (i.e., people will set their search criteria or filter their results by smokers vs. nonsmokers, height requirements, etc.). And sometimes, yes, being a bit deceitful about certain attributes to get more views or matches works. But being dishonest is, and always will be, an at-your-own-risk decision.

So what do people lie about most often—and should you consider doing it? Let's tackle this head on.

Height. Guys often go up to two inches taller; women often round down an inch or so. Do I see that as a problem? Not especially. In fact, sometimes lying about your height can make you visible to more matches, given that on some sites users can use a height requirement as a search criterion. Plus, once you meet a match in the flesh, height often loses some significance, especially if there's chemistry. But take heed: if you're a five-foot-nine guy but have listed yourself as five foot eleven—and you end up going out with a woman who, rounded down, is five foot eight, she's going to notice the discrepancy (especially if she's in heels). Will it be a deal-breaker? If you're brave, tell a tall tale and roll the dice.

Age. Because sites usually require you to list a desired age range for your match, listing your age can start to feel like a problem, especially as you get older. For instance, a lot of men looking for women will place their upper limit at fifty years old, meaning if you're a spry fifty-one-year-old woman, you risk never being seen by a pretty big subset of men who might be great matches. My solution? Before you fudge your age, try messaging men even if you're just outside of what they're looking for. Most of the time, in spite of what they've stated, those couple of years won't make a difference. But whether you're a man or a woman determined to increase your visibility, changing your age plus or minus two years is acceptable—as long as you're willing to come clean early on in a relationship.

Body type. Sites give you a range of options when listing your body type, which includes (but isn't limited to) slender, athletic and toned, average, a few extra pounds, Rubenesque, curvy, overweight, and so on. Whether or not you've told the truth in this listing (perhaps more than in any other) is going to be immediately apparent to anyone you're meeting for the first time. If you fluctuate the truth, be ready to face any consequences.

Smoking. If you smoke, you smoke. Plain and simple. No matter how much Febreeze and mouthwash you use, the fact that you puff like a chimney will eventually become clear to a match, and that revelation won't necessarily be pretty if you've claimed that you abstain or haven't been forthcoming.

Drinking. No matter your drinking habits, listing yourself as a "social drinker" is your safest bet, given that the label can cover everything from partier to occasional imbiber and is the most relatable of the labels offered. If you're a teetotaler, feel free to say so—but know that those who state that they don't drink can receive fewer messages than those who do, according to some data. As long as you're comfortable in a bar without an alcoholic beverage in hand, my advice is to leave that section blank to avoid the chance of being skipped over, and tackle your teetotaling ways when the topic arises.

Location. There's only one reason to be less than honest about where you live: if you're based in a small town and all of your matches have seemingly dried up. Of course, first you should expand the search radius in your settings to bring up new people. But if you've exhausted that option and are still feeling out of luck, try changing your location to the nearest larger town or city that's within reasonable driving distance. Just be willing to explain your location—and hop in your car—if and when it's time to meet up.

Relationship status. Single is single. Divorced is not single—it's divorced. Be forthcoming about your past; if you meet someone in person, he or she is going to find out about your relationships of yore eventually. There's no need to look like a liar over something you can't change.

There are certain questions or prompts—beyond those that I just talked about—that give people pause. These aren't always a simple matter of something factual but also fudge-able, such as height; rather, these prompts delve into the realm of personal beliefs and objectively unarguable truths. The issue then becomes not whether you want to lie (because it would undoubtedly be detrimental) but rather whether you really want to disclose that information. Let's break it down.

Weight. Only a few sites ask you to straight up tell the world how much you weigh (JDate, lookin' at you . . .). If you're on one of them, for the love of God, just leave it blank. Asking for your weight is rude—a number that you're rarely, if ever, going to share with a significant other, let alone on a first date or to a total stranger. Stick to answering the "body type" prompt and leave it at that.

Religion, faith, and/or political views. Are these beliefs a core part of who you are? Does your stance on these issues affect you on a day-to-day basis? Is it important to you that a match have the same ideals as you or at least will accept your steadfast stance? If so, go ahead and list these topics. But if these beliefs aren't deal-breakers, leaving these prompts blank opens you up to a larger pool of potential matches—and you can deal with your agreements or disagreements on these topics as an in-person relationship progresses.

Level of education. If you leave this question blank, people assume the worst. List your highest level of education—and own it. If you're not especially proud of your schooling, make a point of showing off your smarts and ambition when you write about yourself.

Income. This is a tricky topic for a lot of reasons, but namely because no matter where you fall on the earning spectrum, posting your income can either attract or repel people. This is why, for the most part, I recommend leaving it blank. That being said, especially if you make a good living, sometimes it can be a boon to list your cash flow, as long as it's paired with a smart, authentic personal page. Yes, you run the risk of attracting people who are more interested in your money than in you, but there's no point in denying that you might attract some quality people who wouldn't have necessarily taken notice if it weren't for your status. What's more, especially if you're female, listing your income can be a way to weed out guys who are scared off by a woman who makes a decent living and would therefore be a waste of your time. The bottom line here is that there is no right answer. Do what feels right to you.

Children. Whether you *want* children or not is up to you to disclose. But if you *have* children, you should say so. You may think that the fact that you have a three-year-old is going to deter some matches—and (news flash!) it might. But when you have a kid and take care of him or her fully or a large part of the time, this information is absolutely essential. You may think that going out with someone a few times before revealing your parenthood will mean that person will become attached enough to you to overlook your offspring, but what's more likely is that you're setting yourself up for heartbreak. Disclose upfront, and you'll find the people who are either in the same boat, or supportive from the beginning.

Ethnicity. Most sites give you the ability to search for your matches by a variety of criteria, race/ethnicity being one of them. If the idea of being sought out purely based on your heritage makes you uncomfortable, don't hesitate to leave this section blank.

Drugs. If you don't do drugs of any kind, then great! Say precisely that— if you want to. But beyond abstaining completely, this question gets murky. What's considered a drug? Is marijuana a drug, or is this question only referring to harder substances? My advice is that if you're a pot smoker, leave this section blank. And if you're into drugs beyond weed, it's up to you whether you want to disclose your habits to the world or that's something better talked about later.

OKCUPID AS OPEN MINDED

Nearly every dating platform that you'll join is going to ask if you're either a man or a woman and if you're heterosexual or homosexual. If you don't identify within those confines . . . well, you're out of luck.

Unless you're on OkCupid. Before 2014, OkCupid was one of the few progressive platforms that allowed you to identify as bisexual (POF also has this option, but requires you to maintain two profiles, one for each sex that you're seeking). But in late 2014, OkCupid became the first of the online dating giants to (finally) expand its gender and sexuality options, offering identifications such as agender, androgynous, genderfluid, and others, as well as sexuality identifications including asexual, heteroflexible, sapiosexual, and more.

CHAPTER 3

FIGURING OUT
WTF TO WRITE

*Discover What Makes You Attractive—and the
Best Way to Put It on the Page*

When you visit your profile page for the first time, you're going to find vague prompts paired with big empty text boxes, all just beckoning you to come and type your heart out. But if the idea of having to compose mini-essays about yourself is daunting, then congratulations, you are a completely normal human being. After all, writing in general is hard—and writing about yourself, especially in a way that makes you sound dateable, is even worse. Why do you think Tinder is so popular? Its voluntary mini-bio makes it the lazy person's online dating platform.

But even on traditional sites, some people seem to think that writing is optional or unimportant. You've seen the text that's boring and lazy. Someone who fills out their demographic information, writes what hardly qualifies as a paragraph, and calls it a day. Like this guy, whose entire OkCupid profile read:

My self summary
Each morning I slam the snooze about 8 times, roll out of bed at 7:30 and get into work at about 7:53. Then, I work until 8:30–9:15ish, walk out the door, have dinner, shower, sleep, and rinse and repeat. Its even more exciting than I make it sound.

I mean, at least we know that the man's got a routine, but we haven't really learned anything of value about him—except perhaps that he isn't much of a morning person, doesn't follow basic grammatical rules, and has a sarcastic streak.

And you've probably seen the text that's generic, riddled with clichés and vague and meaningless phrases. Here's what this woman came up with on Match.com:

In my own words

I live life to the fullest and enjoy a good laugh. I make sure I smile as much as possible. . . . Life is too short to wonder "what if?" I am the sassy and sweet, fun, sexy girl next door. I love a night at home just as much as going out. I subscribe to the philosophy that actions speak louder than words. Kindness, generosity, humor and spontaneity are all qualities I'm looking for in a partner. Born and raised in New York. Family is very important to me. I am warm hearted and honest. What you see is what you get with me. I don't play games. If you want to know more about me, Just ask!

The only thing missing is, "I enjoy long walks on the beach."

And of course, there's the . . . let's just call it deeply misguided. There was more to this man's profile, but I'll spare you and just hit the highlights:

My self summary

****First off, I'd like to be polite as possible when I say this because some of you are being very mean for no reason. But I guarantee that if I saw you somewhere, struck up a conversation, then ask for your number you would give it to me. So don't sit there and hide behind your computer like you are too good for anyone and say cruel things and be mean. We all are in the same boat here. So be nice. One more thing, I'm giving this a little more time to see what happens but I've never came across so so many vain girls/women in my life before this site. It's very sad actually. This only applies to the ones that know who you are.************

I'm really good at

Sweeping You Off Your Feet!!!

After that first paragraph, I don't think this guy's sweeping anyone anywhere.

> **Spoiler alert:** No matter what type of relationship you're looking for, these types of profiles simply aren't going to cut it. Not even if you pair them with the most attractive set of photos the world has ever seen.

So when you're composing your profile, your goal is to avoid these (among other) pitfalls at all costs. If you do, you'll be ahead of a solid 80 percent of online daters out there.

The writing can't be taken lightly, though. Real talk: it's going to require time, effort, and energy. But I can promise you that (corny-but-true sentiment alert!) every minute you've spent working on your profile will be worth it the moment you meet the person who will change your life forever.

In the rest of this chapter I lay out a simple, step-by-step plan that—whether you consider yourself a wordsmith or often find yourself wordless—will take you through everything from figuring out WTF there is to say about yourself to how to say it in a way that makes matches take notice. So push those pre-profile jitters and that self-doubt out of your mind. It's time to put on your big-kid pants, buckle down, and get to work.

BUT ... BUT ... BUT ...

People come up with all kinds of explanations as to why they're the exception to the hard-work rule and don't need to bother with prolific prose—even though, ultimately, they're not and they do. So let's take a second to tackle some of these excuses head on.

"But no one reads the profile text, anyway." You only have two things to set yourself apart from the thousands of other people out there searching for the same thing that you are: your photos and whatever it is you've written in those boxes. And once someone's given you the all-clear on your pics, what you've penned is all that's left—it serves as the lone indicator for everything from your intelligence to your sense of humor to your compatibility with the person reading. If you think photos are the end-all of match selection, Tinder is your game. But as hundreds of my clients can tell you, the writing in your profile can be the difference between virtual success and all-too-real frustration.

"But I'm a hot woman." "You don't need a good profile if you're a hot girl!" one of my close guy friends said recently. "You just get tons of messages no matter what." That got me thinking. Yes, it's true—you could throw up a couple of cleavage selfies, type a mediocre description of yourself, and watch your inbox light up like the night sky during the Superbowl fireworks show . . . as long as ur hot, hey gorgeous, and some more, ahem, explicit notes are the messages you want to receive.

"But I'm only casually dating." Therefore it's not worth the time. And sure, if your primary goal is to get laid a lot, maybe eloquent prose takes a backseat to shirtless torsos and bikini profile shots. But with a dumb profile, you'll likely end up with dates that fit the same description. If that's all you want, then by all means do your thang—just know that I can't help you.

"But I just sold my start-up." Aka I'm rich, and that's enough. Sure, an impressive salary will probably garner you some attention even with an entirely blank profile, but do you really want economic status to be your sole selling point? You may have a slew of people contacting you, yes—but without a thoughtful profile, it will be for all the wrong reasons. Plus, your salary could actually be a turnoff. When people see that you're relying on your abundance of cash rather than your cranium to up your desirability, they may pretty easily conclude that you're a pompous ass and never make (or return) contact.

"But I'm cool and I know it." You roll with the A-listers, have the hookup for every great party, and sport sunglasses indoors like a boss. People should not only be impressed, but also line up to hang out with you. With a few fly photos and slick sentences, maybe they will—but they'll be doing it for superficial reasons. When your profile lacks substance, you lack substance . . . and will attract matches who care more about your ability to get them into the hottest new club than they do about you.

"But I'll just send smart messages to people." An intelligent message, even paired with a not-so-smart profile, can sometimes do the trick. But remember, the online dating world is cutthroat. Even the wittiest messages can't tell a match a quarter of the things that a well-thought-out essay can. And most of the time, matches want to know more—from whether you share their love for *Parks and Rec* to whether you'd be able to hold your own on a camping trip.

In every case, these excuses for piss-poor profiles point to one thing: you're copping out. You may say that you're looking for a real relationship, but your refusal to put the necessary effort into crafting your profile shows a potential match exactly the opposite. And actions (or lack thereof) speak louder than words.

The point is that taking the easy road will lower the caliber of matches you attract, and there's no escaping the labor that comes along with writing your profile. No matter how attractive or rich or smart you are, if you're looking for something meaningful, your profile needs to show it.

READY? LET'S DO THIS!

There is, of course, one big excuse that people use to justify having a mediocre profile that we didn't cover: "But I just don't know what to say or how to say it!" Honestly, this excuse is completely normal and at least somewhat justified. After all, it's not like schools really teach you to write, well, much of anything, let alone about yourself, let alone in an attractive way.

Even though I've personally written thousands of profiles, the last one that I truly struggled with was my own. My mind went totally blank. If someone had taken me hostage and told me to churn out stellar answers, I don't think I would have been able to come close to picking out what was important or interesting about my own life. My hobbies suddenly just didn't seem very interesting, and since when had I had so few hobbies, anyway? And why oh why was I suddenly feeling the nearly irresistible urge to describe myself as "laid back," just like every other Internet dater on the planet? I didn't know what to say or how to say it! Truly, I understand the pain.

But instead of turning to Xanax for relief, I put together something much more effective and much less physically addictive—a four-step plan that will guide you through every stage of writing your perfect profile. It's a plan that I adopted for my clients long ago, and after seeing it work for them, I know it can work for you too.

Step 1: Get to know yourself.
Step 2: Zero in.
Step 3: Take a break. (Phew!)
Step 4: Gear up and write.

STEP 1: GET TO KNOW YOURSELF

Below, you'll find a version of the questionnaire that I give my clients. It serves as the foundation of each of their profiles and, after you fill it out, will serve as the foundation of yours too.

The questionnaire starts out by gathering the key points of your life. But if you want your profile to attract that perfect match, key points simply aren't going to cut it. So following each prompt, I've posed a slew of specific questions you can—and should—answer. They're by no means the only follow-ups you should consider; rather, they're simply there to help you start to think outside of the box and to understand what type of specific details will help your profile stand out. I've also provided some helpful hints about whether or not a topic is something you'll want to include in the final version of your profile.

A few pointers before you get started:

- Write your answers. With pen, pencil, or on your computer. If you're thinking about merely storing the information in your head, stop right there. Literally penning facts and stories about your life in a no-pressure situation will not only help you remember what you've covered but also allow you to establish an easygoing, natural, and genuine writing style that will translate seamlessly into your final profile text. You won't freeze up trying to sound smart or funny or whatever else—you'll simply sound like you.

- While this questionnaire features prompts that apply to every type of person in almost every situation, certain questions are going to be more pertinent to your life than others (you'll know). Spend more time on the answers that are most interesting and relevant to your life—and therefore are most likely to make it into your final profile.

- While it may be tempting, try not to repeat yourself even when your answers could seemingly overlap. If you find yourself wanting to repeat topics, keep thinking—or get input from a good friend or family member. There's more to your life than initially comes to mind.

- Be completely honest, even if you think what you're writing isn't attractive.

So gear up! It's time to think about your life and really get to know yourself. Let loose, don't fret over your answers, and—most important—have some fun.

THE SIGNATURE SELF-SURVEY

Background & Current Location
Where did you grow up?
> *Did you move around a lot? Has where you've grown up impacted your adult life in any significant or cool/interesting/funny ways? Do you have any stories from being a kid that really illustrate who you are today?*

What's your favorite thing about the city, town, or country/region in which you're currently living?
> *Has living near the ocean really upped your fishing game? Do you ride your bike everywhere? Are people always commenting on your accent? Does a local restaurant have your favorite barbeque in the state?*

> Hint: Try to frame your answer in a way that relates to you personally rather than saying something generic and widely accepted about your current locale. For example, "I love being able to see Broadway shows on a whim" is better than "There is a lot of culture here."

Family
Do you have kids? If so, do they live with you?
> *Are they young, or are they teenagers? What are a few activities that you most enjoy doing with them? Do they have any hilarious quirks that you feel comfortable sharing?*

> Hint: If your kids don't play a direct role in your day-to-day life, there's no explicit need to mention them at this point. But if they live with you, even part time, it's often best to disclose that fact early on to avoid going out with matches for whom kids are a deal-breaker.

What role does family and/or extended family play in your life, if any?
> *Do you cook every Thanksgiving meal? Would you never miss the annual family cruise? Are you very close to a sibling or three—or are you the best aunt or uncle on the planet? Do you hang out with your godson or goddaughter on weekends?*

Hint: As with kids, if your family doesn't impact you directly, there's no explicit need to mention them in your profile.

Do you have pets?
If so, what animal(s)? What age(s)? Names? Do you have a good adoption story? Do you and your pet(s) have any cute/funny/amusing rituals?

Work

What do you do for a living? Describe your job as though you were talking to a five-year-old.

Hint: Work jargon has no place in your profile. If a five-year-old couldn't understand what you do, you've gone too deep down the rabbit hole.
How long have you been doing what you're doing? What's your official title? What are some of your daily responsibilities? Does your job offer any great perks, or is the office culture particularly noteworthy? For example, do you get to eschew the suit and tie? Are there weekly foosball matches? Frozen-drink Fridays? Can you make your own hours or work remotely? If it's relevant, think about what makes your office or job unique.

What's your favorite part of your job?
Hint: "I work with great people" is NOT a great answer in this case because it's a cliché. What's more, it doesn't tell a potential match anything about you. Get creative and think positive!

Would you say that your work is a core part of who you are? Or is it more just something you do to earn a living?
Hint: The more your identity is tied up in your career, the more passion that you want to convey in your profile about it.

If you could have any job in the world, what would it be?
Hint: This can be real or ridiculous.

Lifestyle

Do you exercise? If so, what do you do? How often?
Do you take part in any types of races or competitions? Do you play on any recreational sports teams or in any leagues?

Hint: Being active is almost always an attractive trait to a match, which makes even just a quick mention of your exercise and/or sports habits worthwhile. If you're more the sedentary type, you don't have to say that blatantly—just skip mentions of physical activity altogether.

Do you drink? If so, what's your favorite alcoholic drink?
Do you go out often? What types of places do you frequent? Lounges? Dive bars? Clubs? Pubs? Somewhere else?
Hint: Your answers to these questions are a great way to get specific in the "On a typical weekend night, I am . . . " or "For fun I like to . . . " prompts.

Your Life
List at least five hobbies and/or interests that you have.
Hint: These can include everything from "watching film noir movies," to "finding the best food in my city," to "fixing up my house"; you don't have to be engrossed in these things 24/7.

List at least three activities that you participate in on the weekends.
Hint: These don't have to be activities that happen every weekend; rather, what do you pursue when you have an entire day free?

List at least three things that you really just enjoy.
Hint: These can be concrete objects, but they can also be experiences. For example, "the smell of freshly mowed grass," "wine tasting," "'70s kitsch," "dancing to salsa music," "Paul Rudd."

After you've written down your basic answers to the previous three prompts, draw out interesting details by asking this slew of follow-ups to each answer when applicable.
How long have you been interested in this thing? How did you learn about and/or get involved in it? What's your favorite part of this activity or interest? How often do you do this? Where do you do this? Who do you do this with? How big of a role does it play in your life? Do you have any accomplishments in this interest or activity that you're particularly proud of? Do you have any cool/funny/interesting stories about a time that you were involved in this?

In the last six months, what's the most interesting thing you have done or accomplished?

What made it so enjoyable or rewarding? Do you plan to do this thing again? Is there a good story behind it?

Your Match

In a few sentences, describe your ideal match.

Hint: Try to steer clear of physical characteristics (i.e., "I only go for blondes," "Must be over six feet tall," etc.). These types of requirements make you seem shallow and close-minded.

What types of things would you two do together? How much time would you spend together? Is it vital that he or she be interested in the same things that you are, or is it okay to have disparate interests?

Homework

Now, find at least two people who know you really, really well. Ask each to list, off of the top of his or her head, six things that you love.

Hint: While items on these lists can include anything (activities, people, places, things, etc.), some answers are absolutely better than others—specificity is key! If your friends list everything on the bad side, ask them to try again.

N-O-O-O-O: "music," "laughing," "women/men," "iPhone," "sleeping," "food," "travel," etc.

BETTER: "'90s music," "board games," "wine," "cooking," "exercise," etc.

YES: "Britney Spears in the '90s," "Cards Against Humanity," "Pinot Noir," "attempting to cook food you see on the Barefoot Contessa," "potted plants," "grilled cheese," "old-school SNL," "Bikram yoga," etc.

Pro tip: Don't skip this step! The people who know you best are perfect for getting an outsider's perspective. The things that they associate with you are often things that you pass over when you're thinking about yourself—and not only can these interests help with the brainstorming process, but they can also provide some great insights into the way you present yourself.

Bonus: Often their answers are easily incorporated into "Things I could never do without" or "My favorite things" prompts!

COMMON INTERESTS—AND FOLLOW-UPS TO MAKE YOUR ANSWERS UNIQUE

If you're worried that your interests are all too common or clichéd, don't fret. Answering these simple, specific questions will help make your answers your own—and make you stand out from all of the other traveling, sports-loving foodies of the world.

Travel

How often do you travel?
Do you go more for work or for pleasure?
Where are all the places you have been? Is your traveling done mostly nationally or abroad?
Where's your favorite place to travel? Why do you love it there?
Where did you go on your last trip?
How do you like to travel? Live like the locals? Foodie tours? Backpacking/hiking trips? Hitting cultural hot spots? Glamping? Something else?
Where do you typically stay? Upscale hotels? Hostels? House exchange? Somewhere else?
Do you have any upcoming trips planned? To where? If not, where would you like to go next?
Do you take any annual trips? If so, whom do you go with?
What's a cool/interesting/funny story about something that happened while you were traveling?
What's the most incredible thing you've ever done or experienced in your travels?

Restaurants/Food

How often do you eat out?
Are you in it for the great food, or do you really enjoy the experience of restaurants?
What types of places do you like to try? Ethnic food? Trendy new spots? Holes in the wall? Upscale dining? Somewhere else?
Are you the type of person who finds something that you like and sticks with it? Or do you never visit the same place or eat the same dish twice?

Where did you have the most delicious meal you've ever eaten? What was it?
Are you an adventurous eater? What's the craziest thing you have ever tried? Did you enjoy it?
What food or restaurant would you like to try but haven't had the chance to?

Watching Sports
What's your favorite sport (or two or three) to watch?
Are you more of a college sports or professional sports fan?
What are your favorite teams? Why?
Do you watch most or all of the games on TV? If so, where? With whom?
How often do you make it to games in person?
Do you play in any fantasy sports leagues? What's your strategy? How have you fared?
What's a cool/funny/interesting story about something related to your love for spectator sports?

Playing Sports
Do you compete in events?
If so, how have you fared?
Do you have a favorite race and/or competition?
Have you traveled for any of them?
What's your dream race and/or competition?
Are you currently looking forward to and/or training for an upcoming event?
Do you compete mostly for fun, or do you take it seriously?
Have you made close friends while participating in this sport?
Don't discount recreational leagues such as corn hole and kickball. Do you play to win or drink? Does your team have a great name? Have you made fantastic friends?

Cooking/Baking
When did you learn to cook/bake?
How did you learn?
What types of foods do you usually prepare?
Whom are you generally cooking for?
Do you ever prepare food for large groups and/or host dinner parties?
What's your signature dish?

And now you've done it! You've written a novella about yourself and have all of the information you could possibly need to write up a killer profile. So take a deep breath and relax. The hardest part—thinking in-depth about yourself and your life—is over.

STEP 2: ZERO IN

From here on out, putting your profile together becomes something like writing a book report. The information you need is sitting right there in front of you; all that's left to do is pick out the best bits and put them together in an engaging way.

The purpose of this exercise is to accomplish the former—picking the most interesting, engaging, and attractive information about your life—and also to narrow down topics that you should most seriously consider featuring when you hit the writing stage.

To do this, you're going to need a highlighter. Literally. So get one out! Your next step is to re-read that rap sheet that you just wrote and highlight all the best chunks of text.

So how do you know what to highlight? Pretend that you're reading about someone else's life. Would the information be interesting to you if it were about someone whom you had never met? Would you respond positively to it? If you would find the information enlightening or compelling, real strangers (who are a good match for you) will likely feel the same way.

Remember, you're not necessarily going to be lifting word for word straight from the page to the Web, so again, stay loose and relaxed about the process. What's more, you're definitely not required to use all of the information that you highlight—and of course, you may use any information at all (not just what you've selected) in your final profile.

So start reading and let these four simple rules guide your marker.

Highlight specifics. What's the opposite of specific? Generic. And what happens to profiles that are generic? They fade into the background. They get passed over, and they get ignored. Why? Because they're boring! Because they can apply to most—if not all—Internet daters. The information you highlight needs to be detailed—in fact, the more detailed, the better.

Don't know if what you've written in your questionnaire is specific enough? Don't fret—on page 50 you'll find a table filled with examples of how to integrate the perfect details into your profile . . . which might even spark some new ideas for your own writing.

Warning: Steer clear of specifics that are so specific that they leave the reader scratching their head. For example, you live in LA, but your favorite restaurant is a small diner in Texas. Because the majority of people will never have heard of the joint, you wouldn't want to mention it by name in your final profile without explanation.

Highlight your passions. What are the things in life that get you the most excited? What makes you tick? What do you spend your time engrossed in? What makes you, you? Whether it's building your start-up, trail running on the weekends, or watching every 1950s movie ever made, what you're passionate about will help you seem like a living, breathing person with a brain—and will prove to a match that you're independent, interesting, and have a life beyond the computer screen.

Highlight your best stories. As we'll discuss more later, anecdotes are a great way to convey who you are without relying on simple statements of fact. When highlighting, pick out the stories that you think best exemplify some aspect of your life or personality. For instance, rather than highlighting, "One time my buddies and I ran out of gas in Germany and an old woman had to give us gas from her lawn mower," which doesn't say much about you other than that you were once irresponsible in a car, highlight, "My friends call me Flash because I'm always the one with a camera." (If all of your stories resemble the former, don't fret. You'll learn how to write almost any story in an appealing way from that same table on page 50.)

Highlight what makes you unique. Funny quirks, intriguing interests, extraordinary or exciting skills, noteworthy ambitions, unusual likes . . . these all help create a picture that will set you apart from other online daters. Whether this includes being able to keep a Christmas tree alive well into January, studying to become a certified glassblower, holding a family record for the longest hula hooping session, or having a deep knowledge of the Great Depression, including distinctive info makes you memorable to a match.

The beauty of these rules is that not only do they apply to what you want to highlight, they also apply to the topics that you'll want to put front and center when you're writing, as well.

STEP 3: TAKE A BREAK

At this point, you should be pretty shot—and there's no way you're going to be at the top of your game if you launch into writing right now. So walk away for the night and come back when you're feeling fresh, excited, and sharp.

STEP 4: GEAR UP AND WRITE

This is it! The moment when you take all of that random information and turn it into a single, coherent, and irresistible profile.

Even though I've already told you that the hardest part is over (and I stand by that statement), I know that the writing itself can be daunting—especially if you don't consider yourself a writer. But don't put ton of pressure on yourself—all it will make you do is shut down. There's no need to obsess over every phrase, every word. You can edit or change your profile any time you want. Take a deep breath and remember that your online dating profile is not going to lead to your ultimate demise . . . but it can lead to serious happiness.

So have some fun! Watch a funny video, go for a run to get your endorphins flowing, crank your favorite power ballad, snuggle up to your dog, or crack open that bottle of tequila . . . whatever you need to get pumped up. If you're lighthearted about writing and are able to let go and enjoy yourself, it will show—and there's nothing more attractive than someone who knows how to have a good time with whatever he or she is doing.

SO FIRST THINGS FIRST

Dating sites often give a visibility boost to new members. Don't waste this boost by showing the world your rough draft—instead, compose your essay in a place where your writing and rewriting can remain private. This means you need to know both the format and the prompts for each platform (or platforms) that you have chosen to use, including details such as whether there are character count requirements or limits. Match.com, for instance, has several prompts for which 250 characters is all you get.

Hint: Many dating sites also give a visibility boost to members who log in frequently and who update their profiles or photos regularly. To get this lift without overhauling your profile or photos every couple of weeks, try simply going into your text box or boxes, changing a few words, and hitting save. Then, if you want, you can go in and change it right back! These little updates will help you remain a very "active" user on the site and will keep you from fading away into the sea of less-than-committed (and therefore often not-as-visible) users.

AND SECOND THINGS SECOND

If you get stuck writing, it can be all too easy to fall back on familiar formats. So no matter the size of your writers' block, it's important to remember things that your profile is not.

A letter of introduction. You may introduce yourself when you meet someone in person, but online, greeting every reader who stumbles across your profile is, to put it nicely, cheesy. "Hello there—My name is Steve; it's a pleasure to meet you! :) Here's a little bit about me: I live in Los Angeles, I enjoy city life, travel, squash, good movies, and a great Old Fashioned. How about you?" No thanks.

A biography. Where you're originally from, where you went to college, where you lived before you moved to where you live now, how long you've been in your current location—while this is all great fodder for first date conversation, it makes for exceptionally boring profile copy. Unless there's something either really unique about your history or something from your past that speaks to some of your current quirks, steer clear. Oh, and 99 percent of the time, no one cares what you studied in college. Leave your major on your diploma.

> Hint: If you do include background information in your profile, try to draw parallels between your history and your life today. "I grew up in Michigan—and yes, I do still use my hand as a map," is better than plain, "I grew up in Michigan."

A resume. Your profile may be similar to one in theory, but it simply can't read that way in practice. As one of my clients bemoaned, "My profile feels like a resume that I submitted for a job that I didn't get." Stuffy language paired with long lists of accomplishments or interests with little context contribute to the corporate, almost clinical feeling that plagues so many profiles.

A soapbox. This is not the place to tell the world that we need to be working to save wolves or whales or water. It's not the place to preach your thoughts on any -isms, the latest NFL shakeup, or even how Reddit is the best/worst thing that's ever come from the Internet. Preaching on almost any topic, no matter how seemingly benign, is totally irrelevant to your profile.

A publicity platform. From artists to actors to musicians to entrepreneurs, nearly everyone has a Web presence in one form or another. Your online dating profile, however, is not the place to broadcast it. The people visiting your page simply do not care to sit through a YouTube video of your last guitar solo, peruse your business's home page, or sift through (or buy) your latest artwork.

GETTING DOWN AND DIRTY—EVERYTHING YOU NEED TO KNOW ABOUT WHAT TO SAY AND HOW TO SAY IT

Imagine that someone's browsing profiles. As he or she is clicking along, what's going through his or her mind? "Do we have similar interests?" "Would I enjoy having a conversation with this person?" "Am I attracted to him or her?" But ultimately, at the bottom of all those questions lies the doozy of them all: "Would this person be the perfect fit in my life?"

Your goal is to answer that single, all-important question through the text of your profile. How can you do it? Apply these guidelines to the information that you just wrote and highlighted, and you'll be well on your way.

Keep the focus on you. Each statement in your profile should be directly related to you. Blanket proclamations about general topics and musings on life, liberty, or whatever don't add value to your profile because, even though they're your thoughts, they're impersonal and don't help others connect with you in a meaningful way. Remember, you're using this information to piece together a coherent picture of your life—and all of the info you need is right there in your questionnaire. Ask yourself: Does this fact help the reader learn something new about me? If you've written it in your questionnaire in a way that doesn't, but you still want to include it, change the way it's phrased so that it includes your personal relation to the statement.

> **Off topic:** Will Smith is a great entertainer. He's the Triple Threat. Actor, Singer, Rapper. Don't believe me? Willenium says it all.
> **All about you:** I've seen every Will Smith movie out there and can rap every word to Willenium . . . and I'm not embarrassed to admit it.

> **Off topic:** Buddhists believe that wealth and material possessions don't lead to happiness and that there is power in being mindful.
> **All about you:** After I read a book on Buddhism, I started trying to follow some of its philosophies—which has led me to not only rid my house of clutter, but also try to be more mindful of my actions.

Show, don't tell. It sounds like an obnoxious, high school English teacher thing to say, and, well, it is. But those English teachers were right, and this single strategy makes a huge difference.

Of course, I don't mean that you have to pen one big, long story. But what you are trying to do is craft an image in which each new fact or detail builds upon the last until you've painted a cohesive picture of your life. In practice, this means that random pieces of trivia about yourself, especially in bulk or a list format, don't have a large place in your profile. So skip the, "I can walk on stilts, really like bubblegum, think that candles smell better than air fresheners, and have a lot of pictures of unicorns hanging up at my house," sentences; if you want to include one or two of those quirky facts, find a way to expand on them that helps a reader get to know more than those surface-level details.

How do you do this? Use stories, short anecdotes, and hyper-specific details to express who you are. When you tell, you're relying on vague declarations to paint a picture of yourself and your life. "I like boats." "I am funny." "I have traveled around the world." Even though each of the things that you say may be true, telling a match these things this way creates a profile that's one major snoozefest. Instead, show. Phrasing and framing the facts and stories you've gathered in your questionnaire in a smart way is critical and can make all the difference between whether your profile is a page-turner (so to speak) or simply another "about me" sitting on the Web. And showing conveys the type of details above, but it does so in a way that's not so obvious, allowing a potential match to draw his or her own conclusions, which packs a bigger punch than being told what to think.

In the following table I show (and not just tell) you exactly how to convey ideas, hobbies, activities, interests, and qualities without stating them in a dull, outright fashion.

WRITING IT RIGHT

How to say it:	What it says:
When I was six my dad taught me to sail, and I've been on the water ever since. My catamaran is my second home, and I take her (yes, her) out on the bay almost every weekend.	I like boats; I enjoy the water; I'm adventurous.
I love Chopin, but most of my classic rock knowledge embarrassingly comes from Guitar Hero. Blame it on the fact that growing up my parents were big into classical and that my college roommate was big into video games. (Yes, I can play on expert. I know you were wondering.)	I like classical music; I play video games at least occasionally; I have a sense of humor.
Along with a bell, my bike comes equipped with a giant crate in the back that I fill with fruits and veggies I get riding to and from the farmers' market every Sunday.	I ride a bike for transportation; I go to the farmers' market; I eat relatively healthily.
I never miss watching the Red Wings play at the local Detroit sports bar, but it's during baseball season that you'll find me at live games. (Who can say no to sunshine, never-ending beer, and a good hot dog?)	I'm a sports fan (especially hockey and baseball); I have some attachment to Detroit; I attend sports games.
My friends convinced me to sign up for a color run 5K on a whim a few years ago, and I was hooked. I finished my first marathon last April and have my sights set on a triathlon next year.	I'm willing to try new things; I like fitness; I'm motivated and goal oriented.

How to say it:	What it says:
I'm convinced that I could win any episode of Chopped, and Amanda Freitag is my celebrity crush.	I'm a good cook; I watch the Food Network.
Stand-up comedy specials dominate my "recently watched" on Netflix, and the MC at the local comedy club hooks me up with tickets whenever I ask.	I like comedy; I enjoy live shows; I'm friendly; I have the hookup.
I go through Swiffer Sweepers faster than I go through old episodes of Friends on a lazy Sunday. What can I say, I hate dust!	I like to clean; I watch Friends; I binge watch TV sometimes.
Anyone who thinks that knitting is lame has never worn a pair of my handmade wool socks.	I'm good at knitting and can make socks; I recognize that knitting might sound like a lame activity to some people, but I'm proud of it.
When I trained my dog, Biscuit, to do all of the usual tricks, I taught her in German. I thought it was terribly clever until my friends started refusing to dog sit.	I speak German; I have a (trained) dog; I have a sense of humor.
After hanging out at the local brewery so much that the brewers knew me by name, I decided to start making my own. A growler of my first batch of chocolate oatmeal stout got their approval, so I've already started working on a new grapefruit IPA.	I'm a beer nerd; I brew my own beer; I live near a brewery and go there often; I'm friendly.

How to say it:	What it says:
I believe that awkward silences are best filled with riddles and that anything from making dinner to DJing a friend's party can be turned into a game—blame it on the years I spent as a camp counselor.	I know riddles; I like to play games; I'm fun loving; I was a camp counselor; I'm good with kids.
Anyone who says letter writing is dead has never met me—I love surprising friends with random postcards and packages.	I'm a good friend; I'm thoughtful.
My favorite vineyard is in Argentina, my favorite art gallery in New York, and my favorite hiking trail in Iceland.	I like to travel; I like wine; I like art; I like hiking.
I CrossFit four times a week, but make no mistake—it's not for the fitness as much as it's so that I can indulge my sweet tooth (snickerdoodles, anyone?).	I'm active; I like sweets.
My friends are always calling me to fix their leaky sinks and install their new light fixtures—and I don't mind a bit, since it gives me the chance to show off my tool belt.	I'm handy around the house; I'm a good friend.

Be conversational. There's something about being asked to write that freaks most people out. They seize up and revert back to what they're used to—which in most cases is work or essay-speak. But guess what? Overly formal language is a buzz kill. You're not a robot, and the realm of online dating isn't corporate America. Write the way you talk! It will make your profile sound more like who you really are.

Here's an easy way to make sure you sound natural: read your profile aloud (and if you're brave, read it to someone). If the words sound clunky, they're definitely clunky on the page. Or do the reverse: answer the prompts aloud as though you're talking to a friend, then write down what you've just said.

Hint: Contractions help your writing feel casual, as do asides. Properly using punctuation marks such as parentheses, em dashes, and ellipses also help achieve this effect. (See what I mean?)

Stuffy: I work for an accounting firm in the financial district and have done so since college. It can be very taxing and hectic at times, but it stops me from becoming complacent. In addition, there is a financial development aspect to it that I very much enjoy. It affords me with the opportunity to network and become competitive in striving to win new clients.

Casual: I've worked for the same accounting firm since college—and I love it. New projects, new people, and new things to learn keep me constantly on my toes, and I thrive under the pressure.

Stuffy: In my free time, I enjoy participating in activities such as snowboarding and mountain biking. These activities allow me not only to be surrounded by nature and to enjoy its inherent beauty, but also to experience the adrenaline rush that accompanies moving very fast.

Casual: Snowboarding and mountain biking are two of my favorite things to do. Not only do I love being outside, but I couldn't live without the adrenaline rush that comes with flying down a mountain.

Be concise. Remember, readers are skimming. Think about it: the information that we consume today comes in two formats, listicle and tweet. A "long read" is considered anything that's more than 1,000 words—and online dating profiles are no different. Plus, a match is likely surfing from page to page, sometimes checking out dozens of profiles in a single session, which makes it impractical to read each word.

So as a match's eyes scroll down your page, they bounce from paragraph to paragraph, picking up key words and phrases along the way. If you're lucky, that match will find those points interesting enough to go back and give your profile a proper read, but ultimately, you have between thirty seconds and a minute to make a good impression.

I'm not telling you to go completely minimalistic—a match still needs enough information to get a sense of who you are—but that novel that you wrote in your questionnaire will need to be paired down, with interests stated succinctly. Being long-winded makes you seem undiscerning, as if you can't tell what's important enough to include, and can also make you seem self-absorbed, as though you'll talk as much about yourself on a date as you do in your profile (and not give your match a chance to get a word in edgewise).

Hint: Being concise isn't just limited to the overall length of your profile—it also has to do with the way you phrase each sentence. Wordiness—aka using more words than necessary to convey your point—will make your page a drag to read and will draw out the length. Remember, from phrases to sentences, everything that you say should have a point and should convey something new or interesting about you.

Long-winded: When the working day is over, I switch gears and put on my artist hat. I'm a musician. That's my passion. I play a mean guitar (and I will make up songs that incorporate your name whenever possible).

Beautifully brief: Music is my passion. I play a mean guitar (and will make up songs about you whenever possible).

Long-winded: The main reason I play video games is not for the game itself, but rather to enjoy the company of others. I have always loved video games, and growing up (even into college) I would play anything with a multiplayer option: Golden Eye, Mario Party, Mario Kart, Smash Brothers, anything that has an entertaining multiplayer option. Not so much into shooters like Call of Duty, though; I prefer something that can be picked up rather easily and shared with friends.

Beautifully brief: I play video games—but only to hang with friends. Games such as Mario Kart, that have a multiplayer option and anyone can learn to play quickly, are my favorite.

Group your topics—that is, don't repeat yourself. Once you've found a few topics or themes that you want to include in your profile, it's all too easy to keep repeating them throughout. For instance, you mention your love for travel in your self-summary, then again in the "things you could never do without" and then yet again in the "you should message me if" section. It feels natural because you really *do* love travel, and it's an important part of your life—why not emphasize it, right? The problem with this is that readers, remember, are skimming! They're working their way down your page quickly because yours is likely one of many that they're spending time working their way down. To keep those skimming readers engaged, each time their eyes touch the page, they need to be hit with new, interesting information. Group all mentions of a single topic together and use that single mention to really expand on that hobby or interest. Then you can use each prompt or question as an opportunity to present something completely new and interesting from your questionnaire.

Format. Big chunks of text don't lend themselves to easy reading. So what do you do? Break up your text into paragraphs—and restrict those paragraphs to two to four sentences apiece. And when they're available, don't be afraid to use formatting options—especially boldface headings in sections that require you to list "favorites" like on OkCupid. Sometimes this can take a tiny bit of HTML knowledge, but simply reading the site's how-to can go a long way in helping the readability of your profile.

Avoid adjectives. "Spunky," "caring," "adventurous," "laid back," "up for anything," "well-read," "spontaneous," etc. When you're asked to talk about yourself (or worse, summarize yourself), these are probably among some of the first words that come to mind. After all, they're descriptors! The problem with adjectives in an online dating profile, though, is that they mean (get ready) *absolutely nothing.* First, they're not absolute. That is, one person's "laid back" is another person's "high-strung." One person's "fun" is another person's "meh." "Spontaneous" to one person could mean cliff jumping on a hike in California, but deciding to go to the movie theater at the last minute to another. There's just no baseline for adjectives. And since you're not there, in the flesh, to physically back up your claim, a prospective match has no idea what version of "caring" you truly are. What's more, adjectives are generic. No one is going to describe himself or herself as a "stick in the mud" or "curmudgeonly," even though some people very well may be. So instead, you end up with a fairly small set of positive adjectives that a solid 90 percent of the population uses to identify themselves. These words end up functioning as filler text—they add no value to your profile. And they make you look unoriginal, to boot.

Cut clichés. Online dating clichés extend far beyond the idioms you've heard before, like "I'll sweep you off your feet." They include lazy phrasing, vague descriptions, and anything that sounds like a classified personal ad from the 1980s. Could what you've written apply to (or appear in the profiles of) at least 60 percent of online daters? Then it's a cliché! Trite statements and descriptions don't just waste valuable space in your profile, they also make you seem boring—as though you couldn't come up with anything original to say.

CLICHÉ ALERT!

These words and phrases are used and abused like a keg at a college frat party. If they've made an appearance in your profile, you're sinking into the masses. It's time to either be more specific or think outside of the box about your interests and qualities.

Spontaneous
Exploring
Foodie
Travel
The beach
Sunrises/Sunsets
Friends and family
Love to learn
Up for anything
Will try anything once
Live life to the fullest
I'm as comfortable in an evening gown as I am in jeans.
I'm either out with friends or at home staying in.
I have a career that I love, but it doesn't define me.

I'm looking for . . .

A partner in crime
A true partner
A best friend
A yin to my yang
Someone who complements me

Keep it positive. Negativity makes you seem close-minded—and who wants to go out with someone who's not open to new ideas and experiences? Plus, what you *do* like is far more telling than what you don't. If you catch yourself using words such as "don't," "can't," "never," "hate," "dislike," "not," or "except," rethink including that information.

> **Negativity nation:** I listen to all types of music . . . except country. I'm not into sports.
> My career is in the Navy—sorry if you don't like that.

Be confident . . . without being cocky. There's nothing more attractive than a guy or gal who's comfortable in his or her own skin. When you write about yourself and own it—that's when matches will take notice. That being said, nobody likes a show off. Harping on your salary, your degrees (or GPA or alma mater), or your possessions (cars, homes, jets, islands) is going to attract the wrong kind of people—or no one at all.

> **Cocky:** People are constantly dying to talk to me at parties because I'm always the best-looking and smartest person in the room.
> **Confident:** Whether it's about actors from *The Love Boat* or campaign finance reform, I've rarely met a person I can't talk to. Pair these conversations with a dinner party and a new pair of heels, and I'm in heaven.

> **Cocky:** Pitbull said it best: "I party like a rockstar, look like a movie star, play like an all star, fuck like a porn star. Baby I'm a superstar." Aka losers need not apply.
> **Confident:** I've been known to stay out all night and go on to score the winning goal at my soccer game the next morning. I just probably shouldn't tell you that I passed out in my bed for 17 hours immediately after.

Use wit for the win. I don't mean that you have to be HA HA HA LOL hilarious (unless, of course, that's your nature). What I mean is that your writing should be upbeat, engaging, and fun. If you can get someone who's reading your profile to laugh—or even smile—while reading it, you've won half the battle. Something you wrote caused that person to have a genuine, human reaction; it means that he or she identified and connected with it. And if someone has connected with something you wrote, he or she is likely to feel like it's possible to connect with you in person.

> **Wonderfully witty:** I had always wondered why that part of the sailboat was called the boom—until it made that exact noise swinging across and hitting me in the head.
>
> **Wonderfully witty:** If video games were sports, I'd be the Michael Jordan of Mario Kart, the LeBron James of Super Smash Bros, and the Shaq-as-an-actor of everything else.

Steer clear of sarcasm. I know, I know—sarcasm is everyone's favorite type of humor. The problem is that sarcasm, by definition, is marked by cutting, bitter, and even aggressive remarks that rely on vocal intonation to convey their point. Guess what? You don't have vocal intonation in your profile—and sounding cutting, bitter, or aggressive breaks the positivity rule. Plus, people struggle to identify sarcasm in writing so often that a punctuation mark to denote sarcastic statements has been proposed several times (though still to no avail). Ultimately, avoid the urge to write something that's contrary to its meaning. You'll leave your match wondering whether you're joking or just a cranky old fart—and that ambiguity isn't going to get you anywhere.

> **Sarcastic:** I've been trying to housebreak my puppy for six months now, but usually end up cleaning poop off my carpet twice a day. I'm so glad I got a dog.
>
> **Sarcastic:** When I wanted to learn Spanish, I bought a Rosetta Stone— but I still can't understand a single word of it when people talk to me. That's what I call money well spent.

Self-deprecation is gold. Poking fun at yourself shows that you're confident enough to admit some of your shortcomings without being self-conscious. Not only can this help keep you from sounding cocky, but it often gets a laugh and showcases the fact that you don't take yourself too seriously.

Confidently self-deprecating: I'm a great surfer . . . at least on dry land. Enroll me in one more weeklong surf camp, and I swear I'll make it up on a wave.

Confidently self-deprecating: I pride myself on being in shape, but the last time I was baking with mom, she asked me to hand whip the whipped cream. Turns out, my biceps still need some work.

Be relatable. Relatability is one of the keys of any good dating profile. People like, and are drawn to, what's familiar and similar to them. As a prospective match reads your profile, he or she wants to be able to nod along thinking, "Yeah, I get that." And you want that too—because when this happens, that match has already begun to feel a connection. This makes you come across as sociable—someone who would be comfortable to be around and easy to talk to. Which means leaving out palindromic poems, mentions of your six pet ferrets, and perhaps your extensive collection of vintage cookie jars. Not that you should lie; rather, it means that you should be aware that especially online, eccentricities can easily take center stage even when they're not the core of your personality.

Talk about yourself more than about whom you're looking for. It's pretty common for people to spend a solid half (or more) of their profile writing about what they're looking for in a match. Right out of the gate, they'll start with something like: "About you: I want a guy who's smart, caring, and has a good relationship with his family. I like tall men and appreciate someone who would prefer to read to playing video games. We would love to do things together like kayak, explore new places, and try new restaurants. It's okay if he has dogs but not cats because I'm allergic . . . " continuing for paragraphs. They ramble on about different requests and requirements for their theoretical partners—but they neglect the most important subject in their profile: themselves. Think: whoever is browsing your profile already has an idea about the type of match he or she is looking for, much in the same way that you do. So when reading your profile, that person doesn't want to spend minute after minute reading about whom you're looking for—he or she wants to use the one and only opportunity they have to read and learn about *you*. What's more, to have a laundry list of requirements for a potential match makes you seem demanding and close-minded right out of the gate. (Not attractive.) So spend at maximum three sentences talking about what you're looking for in a potential partner, and use the rest of your words to describe your life and yourself.

Hint: When you're writing those up-to-three sentences about your potential match, talk about him or her in the third person. Using "you" not only feels demanding of whomever is reading but is also borderline creepy. Stick with "I'm looking for a man/woman who . . ." and "She would . . . " and so on. The exception: When OkCupid prompts, "You should message me if," follow the setup of the question and proceed with, "You . . . "

Be honest. Ultimately, you're going to be held accountable for whatever it is that you have written in your profile—and if you've stretched the truth too thin, you're going to pay the price if and when you finally get that first date. But being honest also includes foregoing simply writing what you think people want to hear. "I don't think girls will think it's cool that I play so many video games," he tells me. "I compete in CrossFit tournaments, but I think guys get weirded out by it," she says. Let me stop you all right there. It does not matter what you do or do not think is attractive to the gender you're hoping to match up with. If your interest is a significant part of your life—one that a match will eventually find out about and potentially be a part of—then there's no need to exclude it from your profile. Staying true to yourself will not only help you weed out the matches who ultimately won't be a good fit, but it will also make you more confident when you finally do meet up.

Ask yourself: Would I say this on a first date? If the answer is no, it shouldn't be in your profile. Period.

Should never be typed: I have a birthmark on my back in the shape of Mickey Mouse.

Should never be typed: My ex cut the buttons off all my dress shirts after we broke up.

Mention work. It doesn't have to be long, drawn out, or in depth, but it needs to be present. If you make no remark on your career in your profile, matches are going to wonder what's up. Because whether you want to admit it or not, unless you're completely unemployed and without prospects (in which case, perhaps you should be focusing on getting a job rather than a partner . . . at least at first), what you do for a living takes up a pretty hefty chunk of your time and plays an integral role in your life. Therefore, this matters to a prospective match. If you're not proud of your employment situation or between jobs, it's still worthwhile to devote at least a sentence to talking about what you do—but again, keep things positive. Make note of your current work situation, but follow it up with what steps you're taking toward achieving your dream job or furthering your career goals. Remember, work jargon has no place in your profile. If you're explaining your role, state it as simply as possible!

Don't reference online dating: Whether it's "I can't believe I'm online dating!" or "We'll tell our friends that we met somewhere else," being self-conscious about online dating, and letting the world know it in your profile, is a big no-no. News flash: everyone who's reading your profile is also online dating. The stigma of online dating is gone . . . and any references to it in your profile should be, too.

Believe in the rule of three. The "rule of three" is a writing principle that says that two is too few and four is too many—and three (whatevers) is the perfect number for the human brain to grasp. When you're writing your online dating profile, this rule applies whether you're rattling off your favorite bars or naming the countries you've visited. Two packs little punch. Four or more and a potential match gets bored—fast. It doesn't matter how specific or interesting whatever you're talking about is; in your sentences, long lists (like long paragraphs) are primed to be skipped.

Glazing over: I like animals! This includes dogs, cats, iguanas, guinea pigs, giraffes, elephants, monkeys, snakes, dolphins, sloths, pigs, and sharks. I don't like bugs, though.

Glazing over: My favorite sports are baseball, football, basketball, hockey, soccer, tennis, and ultimate Frisbee.

Go ahead, leave some prompts blank. If you're really struggling to come up with an answer for a particular prompt, have exhausted your questionnaire, or have simply already said all that you want to say, go ahead and leave a section blank. You're not required to fill out every portion of your profile to have it seem and be complete . . . but avoid leaving more than two questions unanswered for fear of looking apathetic.

Proofread and spell-check. Seriously. This is something that no one should need to be reminded of, but sadly, many do. A sloppy profile makes you look just that—sloppy and careless. And why would a match want to waste his or her time and effort on someone who's visibly apathetic about their profile—and, therefore, seemingly also online dating? So here it goes: read what you've written more than once. Hell, read it more than twice! Then get a second pair of eyes on it. And before you hit "save," copy and paste your text into something—anything!—with spell-check. (Word, in my opinion, is still one of the best options because it also boasts grammar check functionality. Run-on sentences, be gone!)

Dudes, this is especially important for you. When women are either overwhelmed by messages or profile hopping, they'll use anything (especially poor spelling and grammar) to knock a guy out of the running. Don't let this be your downfall! Plus, women dig intelligence. One analysis found that men's profiles that used the word "whom" received up to a third more messages. That's not to say that you should start throwing "whom" around for kicks (you shouldn't), but rather it serves as a reinforcement that smarts are sexy—especially online.

THE HEADLINE—WITHOUT THE HEADACHE

On certain sites (think Match.com and POF), there's a prompt that reads "Headline" or "My Headline." This banner appears at the top of your profile or sometimes next to your profile image when you're in search mode, is often capped by a character limit, and is usually one of the hardest things for people to fill out. After all, how can you encompass who you are or what you're looking for in the length of a tweet? The good news is that trying to summarize yourself is the wrong approach—and these headlines are so rife with clichés and awkward greetings in the dating pool at large ("Looking for someone special," "Let's be spontaneous," "Living life to the fullest," "Ready for a fresh beginning") that it's easy to stand out from the crowd in a good way.

The simplest headline writing strategy is to take a fun or funny fact or story about yourself and spin it into a single sentence. Just like your profile text, your headline should keep the focus on *you*, and shouldn't be some blanket statement that could apply to—or be written by—60 or more percent of online daters. It can be something that's already in your profile, or it can be something you left on the cutting room floor from your questionnaire. The key is to be funny, upbeat, attention catching, and unique . . . and to avoid saying something that sounds like it could have come from a bad romantic comedy or personal ad.

If you're still struggling, channel the power of three by stringing three of your interests together—preferably as an alliteration, rhyme, or some other attention-catching device. It's not the most creative headline in the world, but you'll give a prospective match a sense of what you're into right off the bat.

Hint: Change your headline frequently. Not only will it help keep your profile feeling fresh, but it's one of the easiest parts of your profile to update— and who knows who might take notice.

That's one helluva headline:
- Once danced (poorly) with Jimmy Fallon at a party
- Baseball, breweries, and Bruce Springsteen
- Climbed Mt. Rainier . . . and only almost died once
- Raps "Lonely Island" lyrics like a boss (like a boss)
- The Don Draper of banking
- Will travel for lobster rolls
- Contributing to the bourbon shortage
- Consistently scores above 100 when bowling (impressed yet?)
- Inspired by Thoreau, Whitman . . . and Louis CK
- Rocks high heels—and hiking boots
- Has never worn mom jeans or Crocs
- Isn't too good for wine from a box
- Once raised a baby raccoon as a pet
- Has never seen *Star Wars* (gasp!)
- [Insert Seinfeld reference here]

IF YOU WERE GOING TO . . . WELL,
THEN YOU PROBABLY SHOULDN'T WRITE THAT

Insult any group of people. Because then you're an asshole.

Refer to a woman as a girl. Because you might be perceived as sexist.

Talk about the zombie apocalypse. Because it ain't gonna happen, and the fad is over.

Use hashtags. Because they're best left to Twitter and Instagram.

Include external links. Because then you're putting extra work on your prospective match.

Mention your ex. Because then you're not over him or her.

Reference a "new beginning" or a "fresh start" or "getting back on your feet." Because then you have baggage.

Use "etc." at the end of a list of your interests. Because it's not informative in any way.

Double space between sentences. Because it makes you look as outdated with technology as you are.

Refer to your reader as "you" (unless a prompt set it up that way). Because it's creepy.

End! Every! Or every other! Sentence! With an exclamation point!! Because overeager is just as unattractive as apathetic.

Make cheesy, corny, romantic statements. Because it's . . . well, cheesy and corny.

Fill your profile with rhetorical questions. Because one is enough.

Use the phrase, "just like everyone else." Because you're not.

Employ lists in every section or paragraph. Because too many are boring to read and don't give enough detail.

Write, "My friends say that I'm . . . " Because you're more self-aware and confident than that.

Make blatantly sexual references. Because it's gross and conveys the wrong message.

TYPE IN ALL CAPS. Because you're not yelling.

Mention your student (or any) debt—or talk explicitly about money at all. Because it's too personal.

Reveal details of your medical history. 'Nuff said.

Use more than one emoticon :). Because you should be able to use your words, not punctuation, to convey your mood.

Wax poetic about . . . anything. Because no one cares.

Say that you're looking for a "drama free" relationship. Because you've clearly been part of a drama-filled relationship.

THINGS YOU ACTUALLY CAN DO WITHOUT
(IN YOUR PROFILE AT LEAST)

Whether you're answering "the six things I could never do without," OkCupid prompt or the "favorite things," Match.com and eHarmony question, the following words, interests, and activities are so boring, unimaginative, and overused that they'll make you look the same.

Adventure
Air
Water
Food
Shelter
Fire
Men/Women
Sex
Orgasms
iPhone
Internet
Music
Spotify
Netflix
Sleep
Humor
Technology
A computer
Transportation (car, Metrocard, etc.)
Money
Headphones
Books
Sunshine
Cuddling
Passport
Conversations

PUTTING IT ALL TOGETHER

All of those tips sound great in theory—but what do they look like in practice? These before and after profiles come from all types of people on several different platforms and put into practice the techniques you just learned.

BEFORE

Note: This is Connor. His before and after profiles live here, but as one of my clients, he filled out a getting-to-know-you questionnaire much like the one that you did. To see what information he listed as well as what we highlighted as the most relevant information, see the Appendix.

26 | M | Denver, CO | OkCupid
My self summary
> *blank*

What I'm doing with my life
> I work in entertainment managing teenage clients for a mobile entertainment start-up.

I'm really good at
> skiing, ultimate, exploring, talking, finding music, working out

Favorite books, movies, shows, music, and food
> *Mighty Ducks*, pizza, *Boys and the Boat* is a great book, an episode of *The OC* here and there.

The six things I could never do without
> shoes, family, dogs, college football, music, iPhone

I spend a lot of time thinking about
> outdoor activities

On a typical Friday night I am
> *blank*

You should message me if
> Hesitation kills, just do it

My self summary

I'll never say no to a dumb bet, and I don't think you can ever take lawn games too seriously—especially when beers are on the line. After scoring the winning point in Kan Jam, I once ripped my shirt off my person and spiked it on the ground. I don't even entirely know how it happened.

But lawn games aren't the only ones I take seriously. . . . I'm a Michigan State football super fan. I rarely miss watching a game, follow every social media account, and make it to a few games at the stadium every year too, including the last two bowl games. The Broncos are pretty great too.

Unless I'm watching football though, sitting still drives me crazy—so I'm always out and moving. Spending days at the park, trail running and racing, playing softball, hiking and camping with friends . . . and there's nothing on a mountain I won't ski down.

What I'm doing with my life

Biking to work where I'm an advertiser and copywriter. The company's pretty small though, so I get roped into a lot of things—including many rounds of ping-pong.

I'm really good at

Yelping everything—check-ins, reviews, all of it. (I've used the app so much that new restaurants sometimes invite me to their soft openings.) It's helped me get to know the city well enough that I'm basically a human Yelp for friends when they're looking for new restaurants, bars, and things to do. I love that.

Also: tying knots.

Favorite books, movies, shows, music, and food

Books: *Boys in the Boat, Born to Run, Don't Put Me in Coach*
Shows: *House of Cards, Parks and Rec, Game of Thrones, Silicon Valley*
Music: Remixes, and any mildly embarrassing, head-nodding pop music. T. Swift and Beyonce? Absolutely.
Food: Frozen blueberries, waffles, short rib sandwiches, and pizza is life.

The six things I could never do without

Red Rocks Amphitheater

An Americano on Friday morning

Nike sneakers

History museums

Getting away from my phone

Baos. I love baos.

I spend a lot of time thinking about

Which brewery to hit next, getting a Portuguese water dog, and whether having a weed edible before a long run is a good idea (so far, results have been mixed).

On a typical Friday night I am

At a bar with friends, sipping an Old Fashioned, playing Golden Tee . . . and once, when I lost a bet, doing it all while wearing a bathrobe. A word to the wise: if you're going to wear a bathrobe to a bar, make sure it has pockets.

You should message me if

You're not afraid of attention, want to laugh until it hurts, or think you can challenge me to a bet I won't take. You know the difference between a party beer and a drinking beer—and won't say no to either. You appreciate a guy who will randomly leave you nice notes on Post-Its, and might do the same in return. Or you just want to know more!

34 | F | New York, NY | OkCupid

My self summary

I'm an artist and just started a business designing skateboards. I also make pottery and jewelry, and I sell it on Etsy. I also, like most artists, bartend for extra pocket money.

What I'm doing with my life

Camping and backpacking, hanging out with my sister and niece, and pretending to be Katy Perry.

I'm really good at

Spending time with kids. I love them and they love me. I volunteer teaching arts and crafts at a local organization, and it's fun being able to show them new projects.

Favorite books, movies, shows, music, and food

As an artist I'm open to all kinds of books, movies, shows, music, and food! I'm pretty adventurous with what I eat and will try anything once. I like listening to podcasts and have very eclectic taste in music. I watch *The Office* every chance I get because Michael is so hilarious. My newest obsession is *Call the Midwife* (yes, it's on PBS), and I also love John Oliver.

The six things I could never do without

Art supplies, iPhone, my nose ring, a sleeping bag, sunshine and mountains, laughing.

I spend a lot of time thinking about

My art

On a typical Friday night I am

blank

You should message me if

You went to college and have a job, you're tall, and you have a tattoo, beard, or both.

P.S. I will not answer messages that only say "hi."

My self summary

Put me on a skateboard, and I'll fall—but I love them anyway. I started designing boards in college and just launched my own line, partnering with an up-and-coming pro. He keeps threatening to teach me to ride properly, but I think I'd rather keep both feet on the ground and art supplies in my hands.

Boards aren't all I create, though. My apartment is filled with ceramic cups and bowls, and I have an Etsy shop for handmade jewelry. Point being: I'm an artist . . . and before you ask, yep, I bartend on the side (the perk: I make one hell of a Manhattan).

What I'm doing with my life

Growing my business. Taking road trips out West to camp and backpack (Zion and Moab were last—Big Sur is next). Changing the color of the ends of my hair. Hanging out with my sister and adorable niece. Forgetting my keys. Dressing up as Katy Perry every year for Halloween. Yoga. Lots of yoga.

I'm really good at

Hanging out with kids. I volunteer doing arts and crafts with a local nonprofit—and they just seem to gravitate toward me! The fact that I can teach them how to make a duct tape wallet and turn just about anything and everything into a game probably helps my popularity.

Favorite books, movies, shows, music, and food

Podcasts: *StartUp*; *Planet Money*; *Reply All*; *Death, Sex, & Money*

Shows: *The Office, Jeopardy, Call the Midwife*, and *I totally want to marry John Oliver*

Music: Sylvan Esso, '90s music, and I've got a thing for bluegrass (what can I say, I'm eclectic).

Food: As long as it's not moving—hell, even if it is—I'll eat it. (A still-writhing octopus once suctioned itself to my tongue for a second. It was . . . weird.)

The six things I could never do without
Thrift shops
My nose ring
Cinnamon raisin toast
Kayaking
New York Magazine
Succulents
I spend a lot of time thinking about
At what age did 2-day hangovers after two drinks become the norm?
On a typical Friday night I am
A feminist (though that's a typical every day)
You should message me if
You also totally want to marry John Oliver.

Note: In Match.com profiles, the numbers in parentheses are character-count limits for each section, and only prompts with required writing are featured.

42 | M | San Francisco, CA | Match.com
My headline (150)

Single dad looking for something that lasts

In my own words (4,000)

I'm optimistic, caring, and passionate about life. I've lived in San Francisco for the past ten years after coming from the Midwest for a job. I work hard in my career and have goals that I'm striving to achieve, but my job doesn't define me. But because I work in tech I do spend a lot of time fixing my friends' computers, not that I necessarily mind.

My daughter, Zoe, is my whole world. She's seven, and she loves the zoo. We go there often. She also likes coloring, and I do it right along with her. I'm a good cook, but most of the time I end up making macaroni and cheese—though I've somehow managed to get Zoe to like Indian food, which is my favorite. She's never had a stable mother figure, and thanks to some bad experiences with online dating, I'm very picky about new women I bring into her life.

When she's asleep, I like to have a beer and watch something on Netflix. Lately I've been watching sci fi shows like Firefly and have finally discovered Planet Earth.

Pets (250)

My dog's name is Oliver, and he's pretty cute.

Favorite Hot Spots (250)

The zoo and the 49ers stadium. I also like to be outdoors whenever I can and used to be pretty outdoorsy.

Favorite things (250)

Football, classic rock, computers, and my phone for taking pictures

For fun (250)

I used to travel a lot. Now I like to ride my bike, ski, and hang out with my daughter. I also do yoga on the side to stay fit, and even though I didn't think I would, it turns out that I really like it.

Last read (250)

A kid's book that I'm reading aloud to Zoe.

My idea of a great date (250)

Dinner or drinks paired with great conversation.

My headline (150)

Is *The Phantom Tollbooth* considered a classic? Upon rereading, it definitely should be.

In my own words (4000)

During the days, I build Web sites—both writing code and doing design work—for a growing start-up. During the evenings, I build popsicle stick and macaroni picture frames—both gluing and doing painting work—with my seven-year-old daughter. Such is the life of a single dad, and I wouldn't have it any other way.

But there's a lot more to me than that. In my younger days, I traveled the world: climbing Kilimanjaro, taking cooking classes in Italy (which still serve me well), and surfing down under.

I like to think I've still managed to keep at least some of my adventurous streak alive. Skiing every winter, hiking or bike riding on the weekends, and an annual camping trip with my college buddies (where we usually come back both sunburnt and slightly hungover) all help me stay well-rounded . . . and regular yoga classes stop me from being literally well rounded. And as long as my body stays that way, I'm determined to get back up on a surfboard this year.

I'm looking for a woman who's either a single mom or loves the idea of having at least one kid in the mix. She would have just as much fun sitting and laughing on a park bench as she would at a candlelit dinner for two, find my domestic abilities attractive and/or endearing (yes, some men *can* braid hair), and be a sucker for classic rock. If she's a 49ers fan, I'm already on my way to ask her for a drink.

Pets (250)

I adopted our mutt, Oliver, from the shelter three years ago. I didn't know it then, but he has a knack for singing (er, howling) along with the radio . . . much like me.

Favorite hot spots (250)

Without a map, I know where each of the animals lives in the zoo—blame it on my girl's obsession with monkeys and penguins. But I also know where to find the closest craft beer for afterward, which has to count for something.

Favorite things (250)

> Indian restaurants
>
> Helping people fix their computers
>
> Great/terrible sci fi shows and movies (*Firefly*, anyone?)
>
> Nice shoes for every occasion
>
> Gizmodo
>
> YouTube tutorials (they taught me how to properly varnish my hardwood floors)

For fun (250)

> When I have time for myself, I love finding a good comedy club or intimate concert.

Last read (250)

> How about last watched instead? *Planet Earth*—I had never seen it until it hit Netflix, and now I'm hooked.

My idea of a great date (250)

> Does not involve Chuck E. Cheese (you live, you learn).

51 | M | Ann Arbor, MI | eHarmony

The one thing I am most passionate about
> Boats. I have four of them, and I love to be on the water.

The most important thing I am looking for in a person is
> Honesty

The most influential person in my life has been
> My dad. I always looked up to him.

The first thing people notice about me
> *blank*

The last book I read and enjoyed
> I don't read very much, but sometimes I listen to audiobooks.

Things I can't live without (5)
> My two grown daughters
> My camera
> A fishing pole
> The grill
> Vodka martinis

I typically spend my leisure time . . .
> Fixing up my house and yard and fishing.

The three things which I am most thankful for
> *blank*

The one thing I wish MORE people would notice about me
> I'm a little shy when you first meet me, but when I warm up I'm very funny.

A little more about me
> I'm the lead chemistry specialist for instrumentation at a chemistry company. I have two fish tanks and have liked fish my whole life. I enjoy racing sailboats and have started to do this again since my divorce.

The one thing I am most passionate about

Learning how to do something and then doing it. In the past year, I've taught myself to brew beer, learned how to fly fish (I had always done my fishing in the Great Lakes before), and built a new deck for my home from scratch. My next project: remodeling the bathroom.

The most important thing I am looking for in a person is

Honesty, patience, and the ability to make a salad taste good. Really, I'm great with the grill and make the self-proclaimed best scrambled eggs probably in the state, but for some reason my salads are always mediocre. Help?

The most influential person in my life has been

My buddy, Jared. We worked as camp counselors together when we were teenagers and haven't lost touch since. He's taught me that there's always something to laugh about, that it's never too late for self-improvement, and that your friends will always be there when you need them most.

The first thing people notice about me

My full head of hair and svelte physique. No wait, that's not right. I mean, the reflection off my bald head and continually-svelter physique (I've lost more than fifty pounds in the last year, and my kettlebell routine proves that I'm getting fitter every day).

The last book I read and enjoyed

blank

Things I can't live without (5)

A vodka martini

My backyard fire pit

Action movies

Jazz

The Salvation Army

I typically spend my leisure time . . .

Since I was a kid watching my dad with the camera (I still have some of his early prints), I'd always wanted to take amazing photos. Now, armed with some community college classes and DVD lessons, my SLR is always on my belt. My landscape photography has improved immensely, and I'd be better at shooting people if my two grown kids were around more often—and weren't so camera shy.

The three things which I am most thankful for

My daughters

Cruise control (I drive a lot for work)

A full sail

The one thing I wish MORE people would notice about me

If I set my mind to something, I accomplish it. When I started out working at a chemistry company, I was a salesman. Now, after teaching myself organic chem (among other things), I'm the lead chemistry specialist for instrumentation.

And if more people would notice how pristine and beautiful my yard is (I just planted a pear tree), I wouldn't mind that either.

A little more about me

I've had fish tanks my whole life, and I'm currently maintaining twp, complete with angelfish, snails, and little shrimps. But instead of relying on the pet store, I built my own air filtration system for both—which involves a series of complicated valves and tubing . . . and an old Gatorade bottle.

I've also had boats my whole life, and I've started racing sailboats again during the summers through a membership at the local sailing club. Four vessels currently live in my garage—though until I have the time to fix up the last, only three can be deemed seaworthy.

Other likes: my bicycle, the local Coney Island, walking, exploring new towns and cities, and keeping up with the latest technology.

60 | F | Sarasota, FL | Match.com

My headline (150)

Older and wiser, starting a new life and looking for someone to enjoy it with me.

In my own words (4,000)

My name is Mary, and I'm new to this site but very excited to be here. I love a good book, an early morning walk on the beach, time spent with family (a grown son and daughter), swimming for exercise because it's low impact, walking the local bridge, etc.

Pets (250)

blank

Favorite hot spots (250)

blank

Favorite things (250)

Seeing my kids, a good meal with good friends, a long drive with great tunes on the radio, Facebook, ice cream, working on my flower garden.

For fun (250)

Kayaking early morning; playing games on my computer.

Last read (250)

blank

My idea of a great date (250)

Dinner at an oceanfront restaurant with fresh catch seafood and a movie.

My headline (150)

Once sat front row at a Beatles concert.

In my own words (4,000)

Nothing makes you as patient and easygoing as growing up with nine brothers and sisters—especially when you land almost smack in the middle of them. I was lucky, though . . . the lot of us grew up on Lake Erie, boating and fishing with my mom and dad and running around the local yacht club like we owned the place (and with so many of us, we pretty much did).

Which probably explains the fact that to this day, I could never live far from the water. Whether it's leisurely floating in the gulf or going out for an early morning kayak in the bay, there's something about being on the coast that's so calming to me.

But water's not the only thing that relaxes me. I love rummaging through salvage shops, finding little antiques and fixing them up. Right now, my favorite find is a glass and wooden medicine cabinet that lives in my bathroom . . . but may make its way to my office.

Not that I work in a typical office. I'm an esthetician, and I really enjoy helping people improve their skin (believe it or not, even men love a good peel every once in a while). I'm also an eyelash installer—or technically an eyelash stylist—but I'll leave exactly what that entails to your imagination.

I'm looking for a man who likes to get out and do things—whether it's boating, going to the movies, or just walking around enjoying downtown. A goofy sense of humor is a must (I'm always laughing), and knowing where to find the freshest seafood is a plus.

Pets (250)

blank (no pets)

Favorite hot spots (250)

The local bridge that I walk for exercise with friends, Austin, TX—where my son lives, any restaurant with a beachside view, and my lily pad (which is what I call the comfiest part of my bed)

Favorite things (250)

> Puzzles
> Enchiladas
> Bain de Soleil sunscreen
> HGTV
> Using made-up words in conversation
> Orchids

For fun (250)

> There's a computer game I call Bubbles that, when I play, is like taking a little vacation for my brain. And while I don't mean to intimidate anyone with my skills, for a while I held the title of 4th highest score in Sarasota . . .

Last read (250)

> I'm not picky and am always making my way through a book or two—lately nonfiction. I think of good books like a good piece of candy: you enjoy it, and then it's over!

My idea of a great date (250)

> *leave blank*

CHAPTER 4

PICKING YOUR PICS

Selecting and Perfecting Your Best Shots

Let's get this out of the way right here and now: yes, your profile must have photos—yes, plural—and not just because profiles with a photo get up to nine times as many messages . . . but they do.

Mostly it's because, honestly, there is absolutely no excuse to not have recent and decent photos of yourself. It's true, you may not be a millennial who's constantly being followed around by your hipster BFF with an SLR around his neck, but that's not an excuse. Neither is, "But I'm usually the one behind the camera!" Nor is, "I'm just not photogenic!" Or even, "But no one's taken pictures of me since my weight loss/hair cut/Botox/whatever." Because this is not the age of floppy disks and one-hour disposable camera development at your local drugstore. For better or worse, this is the age of documenting every minuscule moment of life and sharing it online with everyone you've ever come into contact with.

Still, it's natural if you feel nervous or self-conscious about uploading your photos. When I'm working with a client and ask, "What's your biggest concern about your current profile?" I would venture to say that at least half say something along the lines of, "I don't think my photos are good enough," or "I don't know if I'm good-looking enough for people to click on my profile or to want to message me." So often times, they've half-assed the process of picking the pictures they've posted—and objectively don't look their best. So when things don't go their way in the online dating scene, they use that as reinforcement for their original beliefs: (1) that people only look at photos, and (2) that they're not attractive enough to succeed in online dating.

But neither of these things is true—for anyone.

And I'll prove it. You needn't fret—as this chapter progresses, we'll go through everything that you need to know about how to get the best shots, how to make sure you look your best in them, and how to know which deserve a space on your page. The ultimate point, though, is and will remain that if you want to be a successful online dater, "But I don't have any good photos of myself" is not going to fly.

Yes, human beings are visual, but we're also emotional creatures. And we often respond to the intangibles. When you look at someone's images, you're not just seeing the physical, you're seeing a snapshot of his or her life—and that snapshot says a lot more than any adjective can. Chapter 3 covered showing instead of telling; well, your photos are your chance to literally show instead of tell. Your essays may convey the details of who you are, but you need that main photo to get matches there. And no matter where you (think you) fall on the scale of attractiveness, clear photos will help your chances.

So what does this mean? In a practical sense, it means that being good looking is not your most important attribute. Instead, it's the things that make your look your own—flaws and all—and the way that you represent yourself that are going to make you attractive to anyone who matters.

WHY GOOD PHOTOS ARE MORE IMPORTANT THAN BEING GOOD LOOKING

On the one hand, your photos should be able to stand alone. If someone comes across your profile who *does* indeed look only at pictures (as so many claim that matches do), that prospective match should be able to get a sense of who you are, what you like to do, who you spend your time with, and what kind of person you are when you're doing it all, from those images.

But on the other hand, and perhaps more important, your photos also need to function in conjunction with your essays to bolster and back up what you've written. If your profile describes once building an igloo with your buddies, put up a picture of that (badass) igloo. If you talked about being a runner, include a picture of you beasting it in your latest race or while you're on the trail. If you say that you've traveled the world, upload a photo (or two) in which you're clearly in a new place having new experiences. If you claim to be quite the cook, show yourself in the kitchen—or at the very least wearing an apron. I could go on, but I think you get the point.

Ultimately, your photos aren't purely about showing a potential match what you look like. Instead, they're the perfect opportunity to show who you *are*. Or, to put it another way, just as your text is a written representation, your photos should be a visual representation of your life, your lifestyle, and your personality. So let's jump in.

WHAT ALL OF YOUR PICTURES SHOULD HAVE IN COMMON

Just like everything in online dating, putting together the right mix of photos isn't a science—it's very much an art. A subjective art, at that. But whether you're uploading pics of your time in Thailand or of yourself in the winery, there are a few things that any and all images need to have in common.

Quality. It seems like common sense that for a potential match to get a sense of what you look like, the photo that he or she is looking at has to actually *show* what you look like. And yet I can't tell you how many crap photos, in a technical sense, I've seen make their way onto profiles. Dark, grainy, too small, and blurry pictures all fall into this category.

Poor pics are the visual equivalent of sloppy spelling and grammar in your essays. They'll make it look like you don't care about presenting your best self—and by extension, like you're apathetic about your profile. They can also make it seem like you're hiding your looks, as though you don't want a potential match to be able to clearly see what you look like. **The bottom line:** Every image you post should be crisp and clear.

Accuracy. It doesn't matter how good you think you look in a certain photo if that photo doesn't represent the way you look right now, in real life. I don't care if you were fifteen pounds lighter, or five years younger, or with skin fifteen percent tauter in that "better" image—real, recent photos are a necessity. After all, your goal is to meet face-to-face with at least some of the people whom you're communicating with on these sites—and, I hate to break it to you, but those people are going to find out how you look in person. Period. Even the darkest, candlelit bar won't change that. So represent yourself accurately. Shock and (potentially unwelcome) surprise are not the first emotions you want your date to feel when you finally come into contact.

You. You are not your cat, your garden, or your car. You are not the Great Wall of China, the biggest fish you've ever caught, or your home. And as such, photos of these things—or any other plain old *things*—have no place in your profile. Photos devoid of your presence add no value and will be skipped over faster than the salad at a barbeque. Sure, you may be proud of your pets, your travels, your photography skills, and so on—but no one's going to date you because of the way your motorcycle shines in the sunlight. Plus, most sites stipulate that you must be clearly present in your images. So, if you want to show a picture of your cat, post a picture of yourself *with* your cat. If you want a picture of the latest quilt you've sewn, have someone take a photo while you're quilting. Even if you're only shown at a distance or have your back turned to the camera, you have to be visible somewhere in the frame. Remember, a potential match wants to date *you*, not your things.

GETTING THE PICTURE (PUN INTENDED)

Now that you know the ground rules, it's time to start rounding up your best shots, prepping them for your profile, and finally uploading them onto the Interweb. Here's how.

STEP 1: GATHER YOUR PHOTOS

If you use Facebook, the first step is to go there and click on your tagged photos. Make your way back through your archive and download any images that you think are half decent. When you come across pictures in which you're doing something active (whether it's paintballing or painting), snag those too—even if you're not so wild about the way you look in them. Go about three years back in your images before you call it quits, unless you know that your looks have changed dramatically in a shorter period of time. Next, turn to your phone and computer. Go through your archive and continue picking out options. And finally, stop to think. Are there more pictures of you somewhere else? Do your friends have photos of you that you haven't seen since that last vacation/party/reunion? Did someone post a good pic on Instagram but never sent you the original? Well, fire off a few texts and grab those images too!

Ultimately, your goal is to gather as many potential pictures of yourself as possible. The more you have to work with, the better.

Hint: The easiest way to stay organized is to create a single folder on your computer and save a copy of all the pictures that you're considering there. This way, you can analyze the photos as a group (the way that they'll be presented on your profile) and can always go back to that trove of images if you want to update your pics later. Plus, having a shared file location makes uploading easier to boot.

WHAT TO DO IF YOU LEGITIMATELY DON'T HAVE ANY DECENT OR RECENT PHOTOS OF YOURSELF

There are, of course, situations in which even the most timely and best photos you have don't represent what you look like in the present. And if this happens, you're really left with one of three options.

Don't online date. It may sound harsh, but it's just the reality of the virtual romance world. If your photos aren't up to snuff, and you're not willing to take new ones, you're not ready to enter the Internet dating world plain and simple. It's time to either step up, take charge of your dating life, and take some photos that will get you dates—or retreat back into the real world until you're less camera shy.

Hire a professional photographer. You're guaranteed to get a slew of good shots (which gives you the opportunity to change your profile photos often), have the power of a great camera, and can rest easy knowing that someone who knows what he or she is doing is behind it. You have enough lead time to prep for your session and make sure you look your best—and you can enter it knowing what types of images you're looking for and work with the photographer to get them.

Not to mention that professional images signify to matches that you're financially well off enough to hire reinforcements—a monetary investment that also indicates that you're fully committed to finding a match online.

That being said, my older clients often get a better response with professional shots than my younger clients, whose peers are more likely to wonder, "Why did this person need to have a photo shoot to fill his profile?"

Hint: Never use exclusively professional shots! Not only can this become repetitive and make it look like you're hiding something (we all know that professionals do retouching and are paid to make you look your absolute best), but it can also seem as though you don't have much of a life (otherwise, why wouldn't you post any images in your natural habitat?). Limit yourself to two pro pics—and opt for casually snapped images to fill the gaps.

Enlist the help of friends. Almost everyone has at least one point-and-shoot camera these days, whether it's around our necks or in our pockets. Plus, if there's anyone who should be enthusiastic about helping you find love, it's your closest peeps. So tell a friend (or three) that you've joined an online dating site and need pictures—and ask him or her to start snapping away whenever you're together. Not only will this give you options with a variety of looks and a variety of situations, but if you weren't already, you'll also start to get more comfortable in front of the camera.

Pro tip: Even if you've had a professional photo shoot done, enlisting the help of your friends to bring some variety into your photos isn't a bad idea. Hell, even if you do have great photos of yourself, telling your friends that you'll need online dating photos is fantastic. Having a steady stream of new images provides you with more options, and not only do more options give you the ability to change your photos frequently, but you never know when someone will snap that perfect shot.

STEP 2: CHOOSE YOUR PHOTOS

HOW MANY?
We've already established that having zero profile photos is not an option—
but how many should you actually post?

Four is the absolute minimum. I've always told my clients that they don't
need just one photo—they need *at least four*. You heard me! Four. And
my assertion is backed up by data from eHarmony, which found that
users with four or more images receive the most messages. Any fewer,
and a match likely either won't trust that your photos are an accurate
representation of you, or just won't have been given a wide enough
range of looks to piece together a mental image. And if that match is
left scratching his or her head about your appearance, the likelihood of
a conversation developing drops dramatically.

Seven is the max. Match gives you the option to add twenty-six images—
twenty-six! eHarmony gives you slots for eleven. This absolutely does
not, however, mean that you have to (or should) fill all of those slots.
Instead, upload no more than seven images onto your profile. Why?
Any more than seven, and not only do your photos start to become
redundant, but you also start to seem self-absorbed, indecisive, or
(worst) both.

But when you're collecting photos. . . If it's possible, try to pick out at least
ten to consider. The combination of images that you choose, how they
look after they're edited, and the order in which you upload them make
a big difference—so having a wide variety to mix, match, and arrange
can help you achieve the most attractive, and effective, mix.

WHAT KIND OF IMAGES YOU NEED—AND HOW TO CHOOSE THEM
Remember, your photos should paint a picture of your life—ideally, your best
life. A life so attractive that when others look at all of your images, they
think, "Hey, I would want to be a part of that." And to achieve this, you have
to mix things up.

There are five main types of images to consider—and I'm going to refer to them throughout this chapter. Ideally, at least one of each of these images has a place on your final profile (though action and personality shots can be, to a certain degree, interchangeable).

Clarity shot. Gives a clear picture of your face and what you look like, plain and simple.

Personality shot. Shows off your style, your swagger, and your sense of self.

Action shot. Catches you mid-activity, whether it's traveling, wine tasting, playing chess, cheering at a football game, strumming your guitar . . . whatever! Not only does this immediately make you look like a person who has interests and a life (always a plus), but it also gives matches with common interests another avenue for starting a conversation.

Social shot. Shows that you're not a complete and total loner.

Full-body shot. From head to toe—or at least head to hip. A potential match wants to know what you look like from the neck down. It's that simple. Even if you're not blessed with a six pack, be honest about your body. Owning what you have is sexier than any set of washboard abs could ever be.

THE MAIN PROFILE IMAGE

Your main image is your first—and sometimes only—chance to draw a match into the intellectual meat of your profile. Don't waste it! This picture . . .

Should be you—and you alone. Which should be a no-brainer. If you put someone else into that pic, all that you're doing is drawing the viewer's attention away from what's most important: you. Seize the chance to highlight your best side, and don't make that person wonder which of those two (or three) people in your picture is you. "But what if I'm posing with someone of the opposite sex? Wouldn't the match know which person I am then?" you cry. It doesn't matter! A prospective match wants to know what *you* look like—since *you* are the person that he or she is considering getting in touch with. When you post a main profile photo with more than one person in it, you're forcing whoever is looking at your image to do extra work in figuring out which one you are. Instead, at every opportunity, make it as simple as possible for a match to see—and react to—your face shining through the screen.

Should not be your work headshot (unless it's really fun). Yes, actors, this includes your headshots, too. The fact is that headshots are boring—they're staged, posed, and heavily Photoshopped, and are generally just . . . well, your head. There is almost nothing natural about them, and at their heart they're meant to make you look one way—professional (which is often code for corporate and stuffy). And, "Hey, I'd definitely trust that person with creating financial spreadsheets," is not exactly akin to, "Hey, I'd love to grab a drink and get to know that person." Dating is honest and genuine; it's fun and exciting. In order to draw a match into your profile, *these* are the qualities that your main photo needs to exude.

Should be your chance to own it—and flaunt it. Whether it's your signature red lipstick, your sleeve of tattoos, your ever-changing hair color, or your piercing gray eyes, don't be afraid to show off your unique physical attributes. Be brave about yourself—because trying to conform to conventional beauty standards or fit in for the sake of fitting in definitely won't help you stand out.

IF YOU'RE A WOMAN...

Smile! And look directly into the camera. Some data show that the, ahem, flirty face is just as effective as the smile—but I wholeheartedly believe that a genuinely happy exterior will connect you with matches who have more substance than any duck face ever could. And making direct eye contact with the camera means that, in a way, you're also making direct eye contact with the viewer, effectively luring that person into clicking on your profile.

IF YOU'RE A MAN...

Don't smile! And don't look directly into the camera. Just don't scowl, either. Data says that men who gaze away from the lens without sporting a Cheshire grin have the best luck on some dating sites. Why? Likely because this pose carries an air of mystery and makes men and women curious enough to click, learn, and see more.

But if you do look into the camera, smile—with your teeth showing. That straight-faced, "I'm hard" look can come across as unfriendly, and that mouth-closed, half-hearted grin doesn't show genuine happiness . . . it shows more of an uncomfortableness. A big ol' smile, on the other hand, is both friendly and happy. Combine that with looking into the camera, and a match will start to feel an immediate sense of connection.

NO MATTER YOUR SEX...

Your main image should be a clarity shot—preferably making your face the center of attention. If it happens to be a personality or action shot, that's great—even preferable! But letting matches see whom they're clicking on is more likely to get them to click.

And if you're not going to give a clear shot of your face . . . you'd better be doing something interesting or seriously badass (if you have to ask, it's not cool enough).

Change up your look. When someone goes to take a photo of you, what's the first thing that you do? Pose! That same smile, that same body language, often it's even that same hairdo, pic after pic after pic. This leads a lot of people to choose pic after pic after pic of themselves in which they look . . . well, the same. Even though the setting is different, even though the other people in the photo have changed, their overall image doesn't. And it doesn't matter how fantastic you look in that/ those image(s)—because they ultimately only show one side of you. Which is one thing: boring.

Watch out for repeating outfits. I don't want to generalize, but guys, I'm talking to you especially. In reality, it's likely that you're wearing that same T-shirt, that same flannel, that same pair of jeans over and over— and who can blame you? Because in the real world, it's likely that no one notices. But when a person is only looking at a set of fourr to seven photos, it becomes pretty apparent when the "I'm with stupid" (or the more likely and seemingly less obvious plain white) tee shows up in three of them. So even if you rotate through no more than three outfits in real life, switch up your featured wardrobe in your profile photos. Not only will it keep your pics from looking repetitive, but you won't draw attention to the fact that fashion isn't necessarily your strong(est) suit.

Avoid having more than one picture in which you're doing a single activity. Just as in your profile, each photo that you upload is a chance to introduce a potential match to something new about yourself. If you've already posted a picture scuba diving, don't post another. If you've already posted a picture in which you're on the beach, don't post another in the sand. Avoid repetition, and you're more likely to convince a match that you're interesting—and more likely to keep him or her interested.

Make eye contact. What's the first thing that you do when you see an attractive person across a room? (Try to) make eye contact! And guess what—it makes just as much sense to do this online as it does in person. While this doesn't have to be true in every photo (think two to five, depending on how many you post), your eyes are still one of the most effective ways to draw a person in and keep him or her engaged, even through a screen.

Hint: Skip your sunnies. One picture of yourself sporting sunglasses can add a layer of style, sophistication, and intrigue—but more than one (especially when you're looking into the camera) and you risk losing connection with a potential match.

Hype up Halloween. Halloween can be *so much fun*. Sure, some people love it and other people hate it. But if there's one thing for certain, it's that All Hallows' Eve can bring out the most creative and playful sides of a person. And whether you spent hours re-creating that 2001 swan dress that Bjork wore to the Oscars (check!) or shelled out some dough to have the most elaborate costume at the party, your costume says a lot about your personality. If you rocked it, show it off.

A warning: If you subscribe to the *Mean Girls* philosophy of Halloween ("Halloween is the one night of the year when a girl can dress up like a total slut and no other girls can say anything about it"), this is not the time to show off your October 31 photos.

Be wary of babies and toddlers. Not in real life—I hear they're pretty harmless. But especially if you're in your thirties or older, images of you and a baby or toddler scream one of two things: "It's mine," or "I want one." Of course there are exceptions: Are you extremely close to your niece, nephew, godson, goddaughter, or friend's child, and have you mentioned your role as aunt/uncle/godmother/godfather in your profile? If the answer to both of those questions is yes, it may be safe to post a pic with a tot . . . but make sure you include your relationship in the caption.

PARENTS, SHOULD YOU POST PICTURES WITH YOUR KIDS?

If you've mentioned your child in your profile, there's no harm in posting a picture with (remember: not exclusively of, but *with*) him or her—as long as you feel comfortable with it. That being said, avoid using more than one; while parenting is a huge part of who you are, it's not the thing that comes first in your romantic life initially . . . and matches want to see who and what you are aside from a proud mom or dad.

Stay (mostly) sober. Especially when you're young, it's easy to click through your Facebook photos and find that 80 percent of them feature you right before, during, or after the bar or da club. When you're drinking, suddenly everyone from the kid you just met to the designated driver has busted out a camera to capture not only the group shots of everyone dressed to the nines, but also the shenanigans that have ensued since that third round of shots.

But even if partying is what defines you, even if partying is the *only* thing that you do for fun (which . . . well, let's hope it's not), putting your drunk face front and center simply isn't attractive.

Make your pet the picture perfect partner. Everyone loves a cute animal. They make people go "awwwww," and that warm, fuzzy emotion likely transfers over to looking at you, too. If you have a good picture with a pet or other adorable animal (Koalas? Yes.), use it.

Smile. "I don't really smile in my pics because I try to look cool," is a thing I've heard from a number of my clients—especially dudes. Well, guess what. You don't look cool . . . you look cold and unwelcoming, especially when your scowl appears in more than one image. Your photos should make you seem approachable, even kind. So, forget trying to look hard and try to have some fun instead.

Avoid the flash. Data have shown that images taken with a flash make you look up to seven years older than you actually are. When it's possible, stick with photos taken during the daytime.

Celebrate celebs. If you snapped a selfie or had a photo taken with your favorite actress, sports star, or Muppet, post that puppy! For anyone who's a fellow fan, that's an instant conversation starter.

Banish baby pictures. This already violates the "Your photos must look like you in the present" rule, but it bears repeating. The bottom line is that you are no longer a baby. Babies do not create online dating profiles. Even if you were as adorable as the freaking Huggies or Coppertone baby as a tot, a miniature version of yourself simply will not entice someone into becoming your beau. So leave the reminiscing to your parents, your besties, and your eventual fiancé.

Say no to shirtless. Dudes, I'm talking to you. Yes, you may want to show off your abs, but for the vast majority of women, the only thing that a shirtless pic will induce is an eye roll. If you're determined to publicly parade your physique, use a photo that catches you in the midst of an activity wherein a naked torso is expected—think surfing or catching a Frisbee on the beach.

THE SELFIE MATRIX

Some people love them, other people hate them—but no matter how you feel, selfies are here to stay. Do they belong on your profile? The short answer is probably not . . . but there are exceptions. If you're a woman with seven photos, you can get away with two selfies in the mix. If you're a man with seven photos, you can get away with precisely zero to one, if it's good enough. Does your selfie make the cut? Heed the rules in the following table and find out.

	Yeah, Post It	At Your Own Risk	Hell, No!
Everyone	Taken from above (no double chins) With a celebrity	With a friend or two	In a car In the bathroom At the gym Used a flash Used a selfie stick Can see a selfie stick Heavily filtered
Woman	You look *fantastic* You were totally alone when you took it Something *amazing* is behind you	Visible camera in mirror Black and white or lightly filtered	Cleavage shot Duck face
Man	(Sorry fellas)	With an animal You were totally alone when you took it *and* something *amazing* is behind you	Shirtless Visible camera Filtered

YOU PROBABLY **SHOULDN'T** WRITE THAT

Show off your social side. So, you just clicked through all of your Facebook photos or your photo archive from the past three years. How many of those photos featured you and you alone? My guess is far fewer than half for almost everyone. Because how many selfies do you really want to post (as discussed), and how many times can you stand in front of something (no matter how cool it is) and smile for the camera?

We're social creatures. In all likelihood, your images are filled with the people who matter in your life. Don't be afraid to show those people off! These are, after all, the people whom your eventual significant other will meet and spend time with. Even if your social circle is small, it's still present—and showing matches that you have friends reinforces your ultimate message: you're someone people like spending time with . . . and they should want to spend time with you too.

Avoid pictures of you and someone of the opposite sex alone. Chances are, that person with their arm around you is your brother or sister or cousin, or bestie, or some other completely platonic relationship, but prospective matches browsing your profile don't know that—and it's a pretty natural reaction to wonder if you are or have been romantically involved with that person at one point or another. Avoid this conundrum altogether by saving coed shots for bigger groups.

Rarely (if ever) feature more than four to five people at once. Don't make your potential match work to find you—you should stand out from the moment his or her eyes hit the photo. (This isn't "Where's Waldo.") Try to be physically in the middle of group shots, and the larger the group is, the better it is if the photo is coed (fewer people of the same sex as you make it easier to spot you more quickly). For instance, a photo of a large bridal party is not great, but posing with a few teammates from your coed softball team could be. Just remember, if there's one time that you want people's eyeballs focused on you, it's in your dating profile.

Change up who you're with. You should always be the center of attention. When you start to include the same people in more than one of your profile photos, people notice. Sure, your bestie is important and may be in 50 percent of your pictures at home or on Facebook, but if you include him or her in each shot that you upload, attention can easily shift. Plus, a potential match might start to wonder if you have other friends or other people in your life. Even if you tend to hang out with the same person or group of people most of the time, for best results your social life should look varied and interesting.

Don't let your supermodel friends steal the spotlight. Generally speaking, you should be at least as attractive as every other person of your gender in the vast majority of your photos. Posting too many pictures with people who consistently make heads turn as they walk through the door can make virtual heads turn (away from you) as matches scroll through your images. Avoid letting whoever's checking out your profile be more interested in your social circle than he or she is in you.

Go easy on family photos. I once had a client in her mid-thirties who had eight photos posted on her page—and at least six of them included at least one immediate family member: one with her dad, two with her mom, two with her sister, and one with the whole clan. And while it's great to be close to your family (her family did, in all fairness, seem pretty badass), presenting them over and over in her photos made it seem as though she'd never really cut the umbilical cord—and no matter how you slice it, dependency is just not sexy as an adult. A prospective match wants to date *you*; and while you can get away with one if you really want to, generally speaking, let family photos surface later.

TO BLUR OR NOT TO BLUR: THAT IS THE QUESTION

As we've established, you can't be alone in all of your photos. It can make your life look boring and lonely and make you look antisocial. So the question arises: Is it cool to have people's faces that aren't your own featured on your profile? There are some people out there who think that it's not—that you're violating the other party's privacy by posting his or her pic—and because of this, these people either blur out the faces of others in their profile or draw some inane smiley face over each place where their friends' faces should be.

Here's what I say: that's silly. If you're on Facebook your photos are out in the world—and even if you're not on Facebook, well, there are probably still some pictures of you there. If you're really concerned about someone being upset because they're on your profile, just ask! Chances are, they'll care as little as I suspect they do. Plus, when people are scrolling through your images, they're using the other people in your photos to draw conclusions about you, whether it's conscious or not. To deny a match the opportunity to see you in action with your friends cuts him or her off from a part of your life that isn't really private.

And that's all without mentioning that blurring or covering the faces of the people you're with does exactly the opposite of what you intend—rather than keeping attention on you, the cover up is so jarring that it actually shifts focus *away* and often forces the viewer to work harder to decipher what's going on.

There is one time that I think it's in good taste to ask permission to post a photo though: if and when you're in a picture with someone else's baby or kid. There's a solid chance that this poor little soul is already plastered all over Facebook, but a quick note asking the parents if they mind you using their child to get dates is probably polite.

STEP 3: EDIT YOUR PHOTOS

Now that you've chosen a slew of photos to consider for your profile, it's time to improve them. I know what you're thinking. "Isn't editing cheating? Won't matches be able to tell that I've doctored my pics?" The answers, respectively, are no and no.

At this point, we're all well aware of how magazines, ads, and the like Photoshop their images—changing everything from the size of a person's waistline to the eye shape to skin tone—to a point where the original person is hardly recognizable. But that's not the type of photo editing that you're going to do. You're not going to come out of this process looking like an entirely different person. In fact, you're going to come out of it looking entirely like yourself—just like an even more photogenic version of yourself.

Luckily, these days you don't have to be a Photoshop whiz to get your images looking crisp and clean. There are dozens of apps for your smartphone or tablet that can accomplish almost everything that professional editing software can—all with a few taps of a button and without much knowledge of the technicalities of photography.

My advice is to use this technology to your advantage—and put each and every one of the photos that you're considering through a photo editing app or two. You'll be amazed at how little work can yield dramatic results, and you'll be happy with how many previously so-so images are now grade-A profile material.

SO WHICH APPS SHOULD I DOWNLOAD?
The four photo editing apps I've picked below are (obviously) in no way a comprehensive list of what's out there—but in my experience, they are some of the most user-friendly when it comes to making the basic types of changes that you'll need to take your pictures from so-so to standout.

Google Snapseed (iOS and android; free): Snapseed promises "the precision and control of professional editing software on your phone or tablet," and it doesn't fail to deliver. Somehow, the app still manages to be fairly intuitive—and thanks to its popularity, there are plenty of free tutorials on the Web if you get stuck.

Facetune (iOS and android; $3.99): Facetune is designed, as its name suggests, specifically for editing portraits/faces (perfect for your profile). The range of features—including teeth whitening, blemish erasing, lighting correction, and more—is perfect for putting your best face forward, and even editing that seems as though it should be complicated (softening under eye circles, for instance) becomes shockingly simple within the app.

VSCOcam (iOS and android; free): VSCOcam has a huge range of basic, easy-to-use editing features and filters, but one of my favorites is the ability to save photos with specific pixel dimensions—great for making sure your photos are large enough to upload to your dating platform (OkCupid, for instance, requires images to be 400x400).

Instagram (iOS and android; free): Almost everyone knows Instagram, and that's why you should consider using it. The filters are familiar, and they can enhance almost any photo in a way that makes it look as though all you did was tap one button to achieve that perfect pic.

AND WHAT SHOULD I DO WITH THEM?
If there's one thing you should do with each and every image that you're going to put on your online dating profile, it's this: upload your image to Snapseed and go to "tune image." From there, use the Auto Adjust button, and voilà—the app has corrected brightness, ambience, contrast, saturation, shadows, highlights, and warmth. Hit save. Every edit you make from here on out—whether it's increasing the exposure, adding a filter, whatever—will be done on a photo that has its technical qualities balanced.

> **Note:** There are instances when doing this will make an image look worse. Use your eyes! And if it looks worse, skip this step and simply use other editing tools.

From there:
- Crop out excess white space or awkward surroundings.
- Eliminate red eye.
- Whiten your teeth if they're showing. Don't go crazy—just a few shades. This dramatically helps your picture but isn't (or shouldn't be) dramatic enough for a match to notice the change in person.

- Erase blemishes. That is, get rid of zits, cold sores, whatever. They're not permanent—and therefore they shouldn't be the thing that detracts from your overall photo.
- Use a smoothing tool to erase shine from your nose, forehead, cheeks, and chin.
- If a photo is dark, and this makes it hard to see your face, don't be afraid to increase the exposure.

Optional:
- Being in the foreground of a photo highlights your presence there. Use a blurring or defocusing tool to soften the background and really make yourself pop.

  Hint: Limit this technique to one or two photos.

BEWARE OF AWKWARD CROPPING

I know, I know—all of your good photos are with your ex. Or maybe they're all of you in groups or from a distance. When that happens, it's all too tempting to just use the cropping tool to get rid of excess people or to zoom in on yourself. But awkward crop jobs are just that—awkward. And cropping a photo too small will degrade its quality.

BE FRUGAL WITH FILTERS

Filters are fantastic—they can take a mediocre image and turn it into something worth posting. Instagram is notorious for helping people look better through the lens. But it's that notorious reputation that also makes filters tricky—so you don't want to use too many. Guys, use no more than two images that have been obviously filtered in your profile. And ladies, use no more than three. But in both cases, fewer than half of your total images should be obviously filtered—any more, and people will be left wondering what you're hiding.

Hint: If you have a lot of original point-and-shoot, nonprofessional photos of yourself by yourself, don't be afraid to throw a filter on one or two, especially if you're alone in an activity shot. While it's not a steadfast rule, people are less likely to assume that you've filtered photos of yourself (especially if you're a man)—so posting Instagrammed images helps you look social, as though a friend took, edited, and posted it of you. Pair this type of image with a caption about an event or activity (even if it's not *exactly* what was happening at the time), and you've gone from looking like a lone wolf to the socialite of the pack.

This technique is especially helpful if you've just had a friend do a profile photo photoshoot for you. For instance, if he or she snapped you on a run, filter and add the caption "My running buddy likes to document my misery as I train for my upcoming 10K." If he or she caught you at the stove in an apron, "Whipping up my famous Bolognese for a dinner party." As long as you're not lying outright in your captions (that is, as long as what you've said has or could happen), you have nothing to worry about—and your previously mediocre picture has a brand-new vibe.

STEP 4: CHOOSE AN ORDER AND UPLOAD YOUR PHOTOS

Some sites (e.g., Match.com and eHarmony) require moderator approval before your photos appear on the site, and other platforms encourage users to report inappropriate, copyrighted, or cartoon photos along with images that don't feature the user.

But once your photos are chosen, approved, and ready, the order in which you upload them—which pictures come first, which come last—makes a difference in the way that a match sees and perceives you.

These types of images should be broken up:

Group vs. individual shots

Close ups vs. pictures taken from a distance

Filtered vs. unfiltered images

Action and personality vs. clarity pics

Dressed up vs. dressed down photos

Hint: Heed the photo slide out. On some sites, when you click on someone's page and hover your cursor over the main image, three or more of the following images slide out in a horizontal line. You especially want to organize these first three (or more) pictures in a way that's both flattering and attention catching.

When you're uploading, it's okay if you don't think your images are perfect. Of course, not everyone has the same photos or types of photos of themselves—and each of the rules above is more like a guideline. Sometimes you have to work with what you have, and you end up breaking a few of those rules. Ultimately, though, all you need is a set of four to seven images that paint a picture of who you are. And remember, you can always delete or swap them out at any point.

STEP 5: CREATE CAPTIVATING CAPTIONS

Captions aren't always necessary—and can actually detract from your profile if you don't do them right. Honestly, your safest bet is to leave them blank. That being said, a good caption can continue to add personality and bring in new information. So if you do decide to venture into caption territory, follow these guidelines.

Don't:

- Be extremely matter of fact. ("Enjoying a good meal.")
- State the obvious. That is, repeat information that's clear from the image itself. ("At a baseball game.")
- Only list the date or year that the image was taken. ("January 2016")
- Simply list the location where the image was taken. ("Times Square")
- Point out which person you are in the photo. ("I'm the tall one on the right.")

Do:

- Be funny and/or witty.
- Add value and/or context.
- Keep the focus on you.
- Acknowledge noticeable differences in your current physical appearance (usually involving hair color, length, or presence of facial hair).

Check out good and bad caption examples on the next page.

THE FINAL PRODUCT

Here's what a great set of photos looks like:

BAD: September 2015

GOOD: Zero gravity! Or, I'm just jumping. Either way.

BAD: Cooking in Thailand!

GOOD: Lean with it, wok with it.

BAD: Sometimes I like to take pictures with fake, pink cameras.

GOOD: Say cheese! . . . or don't—that camera's not real.

BAD: Hair

GOOD: No caption is necessary here! Leaving it blank is just fine.

BAD: At a photo shoot!

GOOD: We were way more fun than the professional models.

BAD: Hiking Red Rocks.

GOOD: Rocking my patterned pants on a kickass hike.

CHAPTER 5

SAYING **SOMETHING,** (ALMOST) **ANYTHING**

Making the Most of Your Messages

Now that you've perfected your profile, you have one big virtual step left: making contact and (gasp) talking directly to other human beings. You'd think this would be simple—humans communicate by text, snap, tweet, e-mail, whatever, all day. But for some reason, deciding what to say to a stranger whom you're interested in, whether sending the first note or responding, leaves people stumped or fumbling.

This can be such a problem that before his profile makeover, one of my thirty-something clients had posted this bitter, typo-ridden warning at the top of his profile:

> *I don't know what to write in a first message anymore. I craft one that is specific to your profile and you say it's a copy and paste message, I write a short message in the case that you don't like me so that I don't have to write a long and genuine message for nothing and you call it a copy and paste message. I'm confused now, smh.*

While this was definitely a not-so-savvy move, he did voice a lot of the frustrations that people have with sending out messages. Not knowing what to say. Feeling like you've wasted your time. Not getting any feedback about why you're not getting responses. And so on.

What's more, around a solid half of my clients ask for some type of advice about what they should say and how they should say it. I've received questions that range from:

What do you think is an effective game plan for messaging? I don't get responses from anyone. In general, I don't know what to say to differentiate myself from others and spend way too much time staring at the message screen hovering over my keyboard without a clue of what to type.

To:

I see a guy who I'm really interested in, and when I send him a message, he doesn't write back! I try to be thoughtful, but am I saying the wrong things?

All understandable questions—and gripes. The issue is that this confusion about what to say really shows: terrible messages run rampant.

The messages I've personally received have run the gamut of terrible, from the man who asked me to dress him up in women's clothing to the dude who signed his note, "Vin Diesel," to the guy whom I've affectionately dubbed stoned Yoda: "So pretty you are. I'd like to take u for some pies."

But before I answer your burning questions—and show you exactly how to avoid earning a really great nickname that gets your message featured in a what-not-to-do example in an online dating book (i.e., before you fire off messages that will be a waste of time and energy)—let's talk mind-set.

GETTING YOUR HEAD ON STRAIGHT

What I tell clients is the same thing that I want to shout to everyone who's ever online dated: (a) get your expectations in check and (b) employ a sound strategy. If you do, the task of going from profile to first date becomes exponentially less taxing—and can be, dare I say, fun.

Send messages. Lots of messages. I hate to break it to you, but having a standout dating profile doesn't necessarily guarantee you messages. It will increase your odds, to be sure, but there's no promise that your inbox will be flooded or even rained on. So there's only one thing to do.

Send messages—as many as you want to and can—like you have nothing to lose. Because, honestly, you don't! There's nothing, not even your pride, at stake. After all, the person you're firing off a note to is a complete and total stranger. If he or she chooses to respond to you, fantastic—you've just successfully started a conversation with someone who could be the Harold to your Maude. But if not, remember that person was (and still is) a person whose opinion of you and your dating profile simply does not affect your real life in any way.

Be realistic. You're going to come across profiles that you really connect with—ones that make you laugh, smile, and want to make contact. And when that happens, it's all too easy to start daydreaming about how wonderful spending time with that someone must be. Well, stop. Jumping into romantic fantasies and pretending to know the person behind the profile adds an entirely new layer of pressure to the equation. Not only is it harder to craft a message when you feel like you're writing to your soul mate, but if that person, for whatever reason, doesn't respond to you, the snub feels that much worse. So don't count your chickens. Be enthusiastic about making contact with someone and getting to know his or her real-life personality, but remember messages are only the first step.

YOU HAVE TO SAY SOMETHING—GOOD

Sending a first message that gets a response: Since you (yes, all of you) are going to be boldly and unabashedly sending messages out into the online dating world, it's time to talk strategy. First things first: a good first note—one that's likely to receive a response—does precisely four things.

1. **It catches your prospective match's attention.** You don't want to be just another message in the masses. Strive to make an impression.

2. **It proves that you read that person's profile.** After all, he or she spent time and effort crafting that profile in much the same way you have. Neglecting to show someone that you've invested a few short minutes of your own time and energy into getting to know his or her virtual identity beyond the photos is borderline insulting.

3. **It makes someone comfortable.** Just like in your profile, you want to be relatable—not leave the recipient confused, alienated, or worse.

4. **It asks an open-ended question.** That is, a question that can't be answered with a "yes" or "no" and instead gives the recipient an immediate avenue to say something in return.

HOW TO DO IT

I'm not going to give you a true template—one that will let you fire off hundreds of impersonal messages a day without putting in any thought or effort or pressing more keys than the copy and paste. What I am going to do is give you an easy-to-follow formula that you can apply to almost any profile that you come across, then give you examples of messages that are almost certain to get a response.

THE STEP-BY-STEP

1. Read the profile. I can't believe that I have to say this, but I do. Yes, you MUST read your prospective match's profile. Don't only look at his or her photos. Don't skim the text. Take a few short minutes, focus your brain, and closely read what the person you're interested in put time and effort into writing.

2. Figure out what you like about the profile. What caught your attention? Do you have similar taste in music? Have you both traveled to the same location? Are you impressed by his or her wit? There are topics or interests drawing you to this particular person's profile, and now is the time to identify them.

Hint: While you can (and should) absolutely look at photos to learn about your match, if the only thing that you can come up with is, "She's/he's hot," you're probably not going to fare so well.

3. Pick 1 specific detail or topic from the profile and latch onto it. Now ask yourself: What experience or experiences do I have with the topic or detail that I've latched onto? How can I genuinely relate to it? What else do I want to know about this person's experience? **Hint:** Although it's not necessarily ideal, if your prospective match has a really interesting photo that piques your interest, it's okay to pick something from that image as your detail or topic.

4. Type something. You have two options here. You can either (a) write an interesting statement about your own experience with said topic or interest, then follow it up with an open-ended question that's either directly related to your first statement or is about something else in the profile, or (b) jump right into asking an open-ended question.

Hint: Option A is ideal—it gives you a chance to showcase your personality in a way that a simple question can't. (See "Strong Starts," page 118.)

5. Read your message out loud. If it sounds weird aloud, it's even weirder to read on the page. Even more so than in your profile, sounding conversational (to, you know, start a conversation) is key.

6. Proofread and spell-check. And let's talk grammar and spelling. Remember: "u" is not an acceptable substitute for "you," there's a difference between "its" and "it's," and typing almost any word into Google will give you both the definition and correct your spelling.

7. Hit send. And (this is important) don't think about that message again. Do not look at your outbox and obsess over whether you've said the right thing; do not check to see if the recipient has been online. Forget about that note—and keep on keepin' on.

THE WAY TO WORD IT

Skip the introduction. No "hi," "hello," or "hey there." Just jump right into the meat of what you want to say.

Use humor and showcase your wit. Humor is attention catching, smarts are sexy, and showing off your personality is more likely to make a match take notice. If funny isn't your thing, stay upbeat and positive.

Be genuine—and don't force it. This is your first chance to make an impression—don't waste it trying to sound like someone or something you're not. Yes, you want to get a response, but only if the person on the other end would truly be interested in the real you. Statements you make and questions you ask should (at the risk of sounding cheesy) come from the heart. When you spend too much time trying to make yourself seem a certain way, whether it's intellectual or witty or cool or whatever, more often than not it comes off as awkward, forced, and generally just kind of weird.

Forced: You're adorable. So adorable, in fact, that I am going to adopt you as my new little sister. Don't worry, we'll spend all our time together drinking Kool-Aid and climbing trees. Actually you seem like a pretty cool person, I'd love to get together sometime and will let you cook for me, ha ha. Wait! You're not crazy, are you?

Limit your first message to two to three sentences. Four is max, and even that's pushing it. One sentence is not likely to catch the person's attention or make a big enough impression. More than four will look like you are trying too hard.

Just imagine receiving this message:

Not going to lie, but I did a bit of creeping. I'm obviously really into running, and I just had to see your marathon time. The good news is, I'm very impressed. 3:49 is a very good time and I hope you're proud of yourself! I assume this was your 5th marathon, and that you haven't run one since October? I'm very sad that I cannot run Chicago, but one of my oldest friends is getting married in Illinois the night prior. I've done crazy things prior to and following marathons, but I don't think I could pull this one off. What I mean by that is that I drink pretty heavily the night before every half marathon. I find myself having to explain the concept of ingesting liquid carbs in the form of beer more often than you'd think. No, I do not feel too hungover, and yes I am dehydrated but I have a lot of water stops mid-race so that's a non-issue. Sometimes, people understand it, and some people need to see it to believe it.

Anyways . . . outside of running . . . food. I love it. Part of the reason I run is food. I can eat whatever the heck I want unless I'm training for something I really care about. Otherwise, I'll go to town on pizza, steaks, and anything else I want.

It's good to see that you're happy with your job now. I'm an engineer, but I do know a thing or two about real estate. My company is one of the largest landowners, and I'm the one who says how much property we need to buy and provide justification in the form of a design and calculations. I love my job.

Do you have any fun plans for New Year's Eve? Any races coming up?

How quickly did you stop reading? Because if it hadn't been so absurd (read: funny), I can't imagine making it through the first paragraph—and my guess is that you agree.

Sign your first name at the end of your message, but don't give a sign off. No "all best," "cheers," or even "I hope to hear from you." Just your first name. Not only does a first name remind the person who's receiving the message that you're a real human, but it also signifies that you're opening up to him or her, providing a piece of information that the online dating world at large doesn't have access to. It also allows that person to start his or her response with a "hey Your Name," which is much more personal, and makes that person more likely to disclose his or her first name as well, enhancing the feeling of connection.

Spend no longer than five minutes composing. If you spend any more time, you're not only putting too much pressure on that message and setting yourself up for a bigger disappointment if you don't hear back, but you're also more likely to feel like you've wasted your time with online dating as a whole, since you'll be drained by the whole process. Plus, this isn't Proust. Your goal is not necessarily to blow someone away with your beautiful prose—it's simply to receive a positive response. Write accordingly.

Think before you send. Could whatever you've typed be construed as offensive, gross, or creepy—even if you don't necessarily mean it that way? The receiver of your message isn't in your head and (sadly) often isn't likely to give you the benefit of the doubt. Err on the side of caution.

Missed the mark: Hmm . . . I don't know, you might be one of those girls who likes to break things when you get mad. Lol

Really missed the mark: I think you're neat. Like the kind of neat where if you turned out to be crazy (let's be serious, you kind of look it), I would probably still take you out on a date. Anyway you seem like a pretty cool person, I'd love to get together sometime and let me buy you a beer.

STRONG STARTS

So you have the strategies down pat—but what do they look like in practice? Let's say that you're reading a profile and you've learned the following things about this hypothetical woman: (1) She just finished her first marathon. (2) She goes camping with friends in the summers. (3) She likes photography. (4) She works as a teacher. (5) She plays fantasy football. (6) She has a photo on skis. (7) She has a photo drinking a Bloody Mary that's topped with a hamburger.

You could say anything along the lines of what's below about a single one of her topics or interests:

- Which marathon did you run? I've always dreamed about finishing the one in Big Sur after I camped there a couple of years ago, but have only managed 5Ks so far.
- No matter how many times I set up my tent, it takes me at least three attempts before I get it right. I swear it's cursed. Where's your usual camping spot?
- I just bought a new Nikon SLR, but I'm still in the process of learning to use it (think: a lot of blurry pictures of my front yard). What kind of camera do you have?
- I asked my high school English teacher to prom (mostly) as a joke. Suffice it to say that I went stag. What do you teach?
- The first year that I played fantasy football, I filled my team exclusively with players whose last name was "Wilson." Turns out, Wilsons aren't great at football. How'd you do in your league?
- The last time I got on skis, I rode up the chair lift and rolled my way down the hill. How long did it take you before you could stay upright?
- The only thing that ever topped my Bloody Mary was an old celery stick! Especially since it's my favorite brunch drink, I definitely feel gipped. Where'd you get that monster?

Or you could combine two of her interests to form one cohesive message:

- My favorite thing about camping is smelling like campfire afterward. Do you take many photos while you're out in the woods? I feel like I always manage to forget my camera.

- I hope you snagged that Bloody Mary after your marathon. A gigantic brunch seems like the perfect recovery meal to me. What's your favorite thing about being a teacher?

And If You Were Going to . . . Well, You Probably Shouldn't Write That:
- Include your phone number and ask someone to text and/or call you right out of the gate.
- Forego a conversation completely and simply ask someone out.
- Summarize yourself or rehash information that's in your profile.
- Be overtly sexual.
- Comment on the way someone looks.
- Only compliment someone's appearance—or even compliment someone's appearance at all. Zero is ideal; one compliment is the max.
- Ask more than two questions (you don't want the person to feel like he or she is being interviewed).
- Tell someone to check out your profile (it's implied that if that person is interested, that's what he or she's going to do).

MISGUIDED GREETINGS

These three all-too-common contact strategies only guarantee one thing: that your odds of receiving a reply are slim to nil.

THE LONE "HI"

Messages that only read "hi," "sup," or, worst, "wats up," plus or minus an oh-so-flattering adjective or noun ("gorgeous," "sexy," "stud," and so on) fill up inboxes faster than paparazzi swarm the Kardashians. But this greeting ain't gonna cut it. Why? It's not just that it's lazy (really, really lazy) or even that it violates every rule we've talked about, but rather that this simple greeting breaks a key principle of starting a conversation: you want to make it as easy as possible for the person on the other end to say something back. "Hi" puts the burden of coming up with a topic squarely on one person: the recipient.

THE SPRAY AND PRAY

You know what I'm talking about—the technique wherein you craft a single message (think: "So what kind of trouble are you getting into this weekend?"), copy, paste, and send it off to every guy or girl whom you find even remotely attractive, figuring that at least a few of them are bound to respond. This is so common that I've had innumerable clients ask me to come up with a template message for them, claiming that they "don't have time to write something personalized to every match." (Insert eye roll here.) Granted, people get creative with their templates, and I'm fully aware that not everyone agrees with me on this topic. There are dating coaches and even some online dating data that will tell you that the spray and pray is just as effective at getting responses as personalized messages. But I steadfastly believe that in employing this approach, you'll lower the quality of people who end up in conversation with you. Do you really want to end up chatting with the people who either can't sense a copy-paste message or receive so few messages that they're cool with your lackluster efforts?

If you have time to go on dates, you have time to write personal messages.

THE WINK IS WEAK

On most sites, there is the option to half-ass your attempt at making contact with a prospective match. This option is known as the "wink" on Match.com, the "flirt" on JDate, and the "favorite" on Plenty of Fish, and on OkCupid users "rate" one another with one to five stars—though other sites use other terms to convey the same general idea. Sometimes the platform tells you immediately when you've been the subject of such interest and even lets you know who has virtually shut an eye in your direction. Others times, you have to be a premium member to see who's (sort of) getting in touch. And on OkCupid, users must mutually rate one another highly before being told that they have "matched."

But no matter what platform you're using, I can tell you one thing: this move is weak. What you're doing is either wasting the click of a button (sometimes a match has no idea that you've added him or her to said "hot list" or whatever you want to call it), or you're telling a person that you're interested, but not so interested that you'll take the time to compose a thoughtful (or even terrible!) message. This is the equivalent of a big old "eh, maybe," and basically says, "your move." Not the enthusiastic—or encouraging—type of communication that anyone wants to receive.

So stop being a wuss. Compose a thoughtful message and let your "favorite" know that you're really interested.

YOU HAVE TO SAY SOMETHING—BACK

Or responding to a message without blowing it. Your stellar profile has done its job—and you've received a message from someone you're interested in! You're already a leg up because you know one key fact: the person who sent you that message has already found something attractive in you and your profile, so all you have to do is hold his or her interest and keep the conversation going.

Most of the rules that apply to sending out a first message still hold true when responding to a message. You still absolutely want to hold that person's attention, prove that you read the profile, make him or her comfortable, and continue the conversation by asking your own open-ended question. Use complete sentences, spell correctly, and show your personality. And then heed the following guidelines.

Build the conversation. Answer questions that you're asked thoughtfully. Include another open-ended question in your response to the message. Genuinely attempt to get to know the person you're chatting with. As you continue to chat, messages can—and should—become longer and more detailed. Not so long that you're writing novellas back and forth, but depending on how things are progressing, writing two, three, or even (in rare cases) four paragraphs, as well as asking more than one question per message, is A-OK.

Mirror. When you're on an actual date, you use mirroring in your body language to let someone know that you're interested. You know, if he's leaning into the table, you lean into the table. If you have a drink in your hand, she also holds her drink in her hand. And so on. These are the types of subtle clues that help you show what you're feeling without actually saying it. But since you're (again) lacking a physical presence, one of the best things you can do in a back-and-forth message correspondence is to mirror, ever so slightly, that person's style. For example, if someone signed his or her name to close that first message, open your return message with "hey" or "hi" followed by that person's first name, then sign your name at the end. Likewise, if someone wrote a couple two- to three-sentence paragraphs, respond with paragraphs of similar length and number. If that person wrote very casually, respond casually. People are drawn to what they know—and because messaging on an online dating platform can already seem awkward, the best possible way to create a connection with someone is to make him or her feel comfortable.

Keep messages moving. There's no reason to wait a certain amount of time to respond to someone's message in order to seem cool or aloof. The "three-day rule" is a thing of the past. If you're online and you've received a note from someone you're interested in chatting with, say something back! Timing is everything when it comes to taking an online correspondence to an offline relationship—and most of the time, the faster you can go from exchanging messages to planning a date, the more likely it is that a date will actually happen. Waiting too long just increases the chances that your match is also chatting with several other people whom he or she might find interesting, and there's no reason to allow his or her interest in you to fade.

Hint: Although there's no reason to wait, there's also no reason to respond after 11:00 p.m. or before 6:00 a.m.—which can send the wrong kind of message.

Don't be afraid to move it offline. Your goal is not to completely vet a potential match over the Internet, and it's not to find a pen pal to spend hours exchanging messages with. Phone conversations, once thought to be the best way to screen potential first dates, are not necessary. The only way that you can know whether or not there's that chemistry, that spark, with one of your matches is to meet him or her in the flesh. There's no magic number of messages that should pass between two people before someone finally asks for the other person's number or to go on a date—but don't spend hours, days, or weeks exchanging e-mails. Each new message should bring you a step closer to a face-to-face meeting; make your conversations progress with your endgame in mind.

That being said, you have to do what feels comfortable in any particular situation. Sometimes it's as little as sending two messages apiece. Some people like to send at least five. But as I said earlier, remember that messages are only messages. You can't truly know about someone until you meet in person—and when you've spent light years e-mailing with someone who turns out to be not so compatible with you in the flesh, *that*'s when you really feel like you've wasted your time. So when your messaging conversation either starts to fade or really starts to take off, don't be afraid (regardless of your gender) to ask that person for his or her number or to meet for a drink.

HOW TO REJECT AND PROTECT

It may seem polite to send a "Thank-you for your note, but I'm not interested" message in response to an e-mail you've received, but it's simply not necessary. All that you're doing is subjecting yourself to pushback or worse, backlash, from the person you've responded to. Silence is enough to convey your lack of interest.

If and when you do receive an unsavory message or messages or things head south in a conversation that you're having with another user, don't be afraid to put someone on your block list, which stops that user from being able to see and contact you.

The bottom line: stay positive. You are not going to receive responses to every message that you send out. It doesn't matter how good your profile is, how attractive you are, or how brilliant your note was. For guys, the average response rate for messages is around 20 percent—which may sound dismal, but you can't let it get you down to the point that you self-sabotage (like that client at the beginning of the chapter), . . . or to the point that you start backing away from the whole process either because you feel you're wasting your time or you're feeling hurt and rejected. This happens all too often.

In one study, researchers found that men grew more insecure each time they didn't receive a response to their message. The researchers concluded that "this kept them from messaging the women they were most attracted to and led them to lower their participation levels on the system or to leave the system entirely for extended periods of time".* Don't let that be you! Stay true to yourself, stay upbeat, and don't take it personally when something doesn't go your way. Eventually, with enough persistence, you'll find what (or, rather, whom) you're looking for. Perseverance pays.

* Zytko, Grandhi, and Jones, "Impression Management Struggles in Online Dating," Proceedings of the 18th International Conference on Supporting Group Work.

A WORD TO WOMEN

Women can be faced with the opposite problem to what men encounter: an inbox that's overflowing, but a lot of times with messages that are aggressive, creepy, vulgar, offensive, and just plain weird. Some women have even gone so far as to create (very popular) Tumblr, Twitter, and Instagram accounts to shame their Internet harassers. And because of all the riffraff, it's too easy to become jaded and cynical about every message you receive. But for as many creeps as there are out there, there are a dozen more good guys who are looking for something honest and real. Think: almost a quarter of long-term relationships and marriages start with two people meeting on the Web.

So while your inbox will likely be full, both the "send messages" and "stay positive" rules are just as pertinent to you. In fact, I'd say that the "send messages" is even more important. The most common complaint I hear from women is, "I'm not interested in any of the guys who contact me." Well, there's one glaring way to fix this problem: stop waiting! Get out there, find the men you are interested in, and start firing off those first notes. Statistically, you're twice as likely to get a response to your message as a guy is—and by being the first to hit "send," you've already established that you're interested and don't have to be on high alert for creeps. When you send messages, you have nothing to lose and everything to gain.

CHAPTER 6

YOU SHOULD PROBABLY GO WRITE THAT

The Handoff: You've Got This

Since I'm sure that, ever since the intro, you've been wondering what happened to my love life, let me give you a quick update. Andrew, my wonderful first online boyfriend, moved away after nearly a year of great times and unforgettable memories . . . and that's okay. Because after I grieved, I did what we all do: I got back on the virtual love wagon and started adding to that grand total of first dates that I so honestly/embarrassingly revealed at the beginning of this book.

As for my profile, it's constantly evolving. Just like, over time, yours will. Part of the beauty of these dating platforms is that you're always in control, and when something changes in your life or you grow weary of what you've written, a few keystrokes and your profile can read like new. Not that I'm constantly overhauling either my text or my photos—and not that you should be either.

But after having finally figured out both what and whom I was looking for and how to make my profile work for me, most of the disastrous evenings have vanished from my romantic life—just as they'll hopefully do from yours. Dates are rarely perfect (how could they be?), but the ones I go on today are a far cry from the jerks and (literal) clowns that I started seeing at the outset. In fact, the vast majority of my dates are with men whose company I ultimately enjoy, even if there isn't that romantic connection. What's most important, though, no matter how cheesy it sounds, is that with each new date, I have a totally new and unique experience, learn about myself, and grow both as an individual and as a dater.

AND NOW IT'S YOUR TURN

Whether you're writing or rewriting your profile, do it confidently. You learned the basics of building your page, brainstormed killer content to fill the writing portions, picked up winning writing and photo strategies, and ultimately understand how to put it all together to make your profile a knockout. And now there's only one thing—the most exciting thing—left to do: take your online relationship into the real world.

But don't worry, I won't send you offline without sharing a few pieces of wisdom to help you make a seamless transition. So . . .

Keep an open mind. Set out with a positive mind-set. Give people the benefit of the doubt. Try to minimize your deal-breakers. Not everyone is a writer, not everyone has read this book (you know, yet), and, as we all can relate to, online dating can be intimidating. I'm not telling you to abandon your standards; rather, see the best in others' profiles and messages first—and be critical second.

Go into every date assuming that it's going to be a good one. When you expect the worst, you're going to find it. Try to remember that right now, on this particular occasion, you've never met this match—and that just inside that bar, the best thing that's ever happened to you could be sitting, waiting, and checking Facebook . . . I mean, dreaming of you.

But even when it's not a great date, don't give up. Great dates are great dates, bad dates are great stories, and you learn something from every single one. Essentially, it's a no-lose situation. Which is a statement that I know feels like a lie the minute you're stuck on an unusually mind-numbing encounter with someone who won't shut up about how Wisconsin, rather than Michigan, is the *real* mitten state (true story, and he's still wrong). But even if you've been on a seemingly endless string of blah date after blah date, the right person is still out there. Period. You just have to be patient.

If you're really not getting the response that you want, don't blame the world—look inward. Even though online dating is tumultuous for almost everyone, if you're getting zero positive response, something is likely up. Stop *blaming*, whether it's the online dating site or the people on it, and turn inward. Are you on the right platform? Is your profile at the top of its game? Is it time to take new photos? Don't get down on yourself; rather, take advantage of the fluidity of the Web. Being flexible and adapting both your expectations and your profile to your evolving wants and needs is the single smartest strategic move that you can make . . . and if you follow the advice in this book, eventually you're bound to hit your mark.

At the end of the day, you are who you are—be proud of it. It's clichéd, yes, but it bears repeating: you want to find someone who accepts—even likes—you for who you are. Having a killer profile, one that presents you in the most attractive and accurate light, can get you the attention that you need to find a match—but it's when you meet someone in the flesh that the real game begins.

WHICH BRINGS US BACK TO WHERE WE STARTED

Dating sucks—until it doesn't. It's a phrase that a good friend of mine repeats often. And while the sentiment may be blunt, it is to this day one of the most succinctly wonderful observations about romance that I've ever heard. It's realistic, but at the same time, it's optimistic. It reminds you that in spite of all the bullshit that you're all but required to go through trying to find love, with the tools that you've gained throughout this book, one day you'll meet someone, and suddenly all the ups and downs, all the frustrations, and all the beyond ridiculous experiences will suddenly cease to matter—and dating, online or off, won't suck anymore.

So in case you haven't finished your dating profile yet, well . . . you should probably go write that.

ACKNOWLEDGMENTS

Holy shit I wrote a book. Something I've dreamed of saying since I was a kid . . . perhaps with less profanity back then. But you know what they say—it takes a village (that applies here, right?)—and without these people, uttering that first phrase would still be just a dream. So it's time to get mushy.

A huge thanks to Running Press for the amazing opportunity; to Sophia Muthuraj for first taking a chance on me then guiding me through every write and rewrite; and to Zac Leibman for helping me to the finish line. And J., without your insider knowledge, I'd still be lost and/or grumpy in the land of legal jargon.

Dan Blue, if it weren't for you, I never would have thought—or attempted—to write this thing. You constantly push me to be better and aim higher, and your steadfast support in all of my endeavors means as much to me as State football does to you.

Kathy and Bo, whether it was forcing me to the pool, making a Culver's run, fixing me meals, bingeing on *Chopped*, or talking through whatever I was stuck on in order to finish the, ahem, book, I couldn't have done it without your love, generosity, patience . . . and kitchen table.

Thank you, thank you Jenn Goldstein, not only for reading the entire manuscript, but also for always being there to reaffirm and talk me off the ledge; Calli McCain for your brilliant wit, editor's eye, and constant willingness to make me a priority; Barrie Rosen for keeping me sane and giving the ultimate pep talks; and Allison Oatley, Alyssa Reese, and Ed Herman for every gchat, text, and phone call, for being my own personal relationship experts, and for always having a glass of wine at the ready.

A shout out to everyone who helped with photos, each of my roommates, Nathan Bobinchak, and the whole of the NomFew for putting up with my BS and liking me anyways.

Dad, your unwavering belief in my abilities still confounds even me, but thank you for giving me the courage to always keep moving forward. And mom, I'm eternally grateful for every last-minute editing session, the constant reminders to rest, and your infinite love.

Finally, thanks and so much love to my sister Lauren who gave me the best advice for curing writers' block: "Try sitting under the table."

APPENDIX:

CONNOR'S SIGNATURE SELF-SURVEY

You saw Connor's before and after profiles on pages 69–70. Compare the answers from his questionnaire below to his final profile—and figure out what details, tips, and tricks served him best.

Hint: Follow up questions are bulleted; information that I "highlighted" (that is, identified as the most interesting, engaging, and relevant) in his answers is in italic.

Background & Current Location
Where did you grow up?
A suburb of Detroit.
- Have you moved around a lot?
I haven't. Lived outside of Detroit until I was eighteen before moving to East Lansing, MI, for college. From there I moved to Denver, CO, spent a summer in Chicago, then moved back to Denver.
- Do you have any Michigan habits that have stuck with you even after moving to Colorado?
Nah
What's your favorite thing about Denver?
The city takes a lot of pride in supporting and cultivating new ideas, which leads to a lot of interesting activities and restaurants.
- How long have you been in Denver?
About five years now!

Family
Do you have kids? If so, do they live with you?
Nope but hope to one day.
What role does family and/or extended family play in your life, if any?
Family plays a large role. I am very close with my immediate and extended family. They mean a lot to me and I would do anything for them.

- Do you see your family often? Do you have a large extended family? What types of things do you do with them?

  I see my family probably about five times a year, which is good because *I am really close with them*. I have a huge family and see my cousins, who are my age, a fair amount. *My parents love coming to visit me in Denver* so they come out together at least once a year *and we go to my dad's favorite restaurant here, then a Broncos game.*

Do you have pets?

  I do not but *I want a Portuguese water dog*!

Work

What do you do for a living? Describe your job as though you were talking to a five-year-old.

  Basically, *I am a professional personal advertiser and copywriter for teen celebrities*. I have been doing it for about three years. Officially, my title is media manager but *I work at a pretty small company so I get pulled into a lot of things including many ping pong games* :)

- Is there anything particularly noteworthy about your office culture?

  People look at you weird if you dress up too much. It is *very, very laid back.*

- What do you usually wear to work?

  Whatever I want from jeans to sweatpants. Super casual.

- Do you usually bike to your office?

  During the summer, *I bike about three times a week!*

What's your favorite part of your job?

  Getting to work with young talent in the formative years of launching their careers and images.

Would you say that your work is a core part of who you are? Or is it more just something you do to earn a living?

  I enjoy what I do and it's interesting to me; however, sometimes it's just about getting that paper. I wish I could do more with the community and invest in people around me rather than working with teen pop stars I don't know who could go all Bieber at any minute.

If you could have any job in the world, what would it be?

  Community manager for Yelp!

Lifestyle

Do you exercise? If so, what do you do? How often?

four to five times a week I go to a gym my friend started. It's a little different from a normal gym in the sense *it's all about functional fitness*. He has classes you sign up for and he leads a workout for about five of us. It's hard, but iron sharpens iron. I also exercise almost every day in some form.

Do you take part in any types of races or competitions?

I race a bit. I have probably *run fifteen races* in my life ranging *from 5Ks to half marathons, to marathon relay races*. I will probably run two to three this summer and *looking forward to the Colfax Half Marathon relay*. I need to run more once the weather warms up.

Do you play any sports or participate in any intramural leagues? Teams such as kickball and corn hole totally count.

Softball and sometimes ultimate Frisbee!

- What's your softball team name? Is it a serious league or more of a drinking/social/fun type of thing?

One-hundred percent for fun but some people don't realize that on the team which creates some drama, but overall it's a good time. I actually don't know what the name of the team is. It was some kind of strange bird that was always hard to remember!!!

- Why just sometimes ultimate Frisbee? Have you played in the past? Are you any good?

I played competitively in college, which in itself is funny. Always having to tell people "no, you don't need a dog to play" got old after a while. Ultimate people take their sport really seriously, which is good but I just outgrew it. I was really good in college! All region baby!!

Do you drink? If so, what's your favorite alcoholic drink?

Yes—an *Old Fashioned*. I also *smoke pot recreationally but more often than not, I eat it.*

- If you were to walk into your perfect bar, aside from the booze, what would be the one thing that it had to have?

Golden Tee

- How often do you partake in marijuana?

It's sporadic but maybe once a month.

- Any particular activities that you enjoy doing most after you've eaten or smoked weed?

  Reading and eating. I have also *experimented with eating weed and distance running, which has had mixed results so far*.

Your Life

List at least five hobbies and/or interests that you have.

I enjoy exploring places a lot. New museums, seeing what Yelp suggests, going to parks and watching the day go by, botanic gardens. I love exercising (the feeling afterward more), hiking, *taking yard games too seriously*, showing people cool new places, sharing my world with people, putting myself out there, *HBO*, *reading*, talking. I love shoes, more specifically sneakers, hot tubs/*hot springs, sitting still in general drives me crazy, so anything that gets me out and moving is welcome*.

- When you say exploring new places, where do you mean? Around Denver? Do you travel much?

  I try to travel when I can but I don't have the best resources to make that happen right now. I more or less love having an intimate knowledge of a city. *My friends are always asking me where to eat and what to do. I like that.*

- What types of museums are your favorite? Why?

  I love *history museums*. My dad is a huge history buff so it's always been a shared interest of ours.

- What types of things do you Yelp for?

  I Yelp everything. Check ins, reviews, I actually have been starting to get invites to soft openings of new restaurants.

- What are some of your favorite yard games? When do you play them? With whom?

  Kan Jam and spike ball for sure. Hitting the park is a pretty big part of life in Denver, so this park nearby called Cheesman is where I usually go.

- What do you mean when you say that you take them too seriously? Tell me about a time when you went overboard.

  When beers are on the line, I don't know if you can ever take things too seriously. . . . *It was the final point of a Kan Jam and I scored with winning point and proceeded to rip my shirt off my person by tearing it straight down the middle then spiking it on the ground. I'm not sure how it even happened.*

- What do you watch on HBO?

  Silicon Valley, *Game of Thrones*, really anything, easier to say what I don't watch!
- List at least three of your favorite TV shows.

  House of Cards, *Parks and Rec*, *Game of Thrones*
- How much do you read? List at least three of your favorite books.

  At least a book a month. *Boys in the Boat*, *Born to Run*, *Don't Put Me in Coach*
- Where's your favorite hot spring? When's your favorite time to go?

  Strawberry Park Hot Springs in Steamboat Springs, CO. I love going Memorial Day weekend.

List at least three activities that you participate in on the weekends.

  Skiing, *riding my bike around to different breweries*, eating out at a new restaurant one night, and *trail running*.

- Skiing! How good are you? How often do you go? How old were you when you started?

  I am an *expert skier*. *There is nothing on the mountain I won't ski down. I go probably around fifteen times a year. My mom first took me skiing when I was two years old* at Mt. Brighton in Michigan which is now owned by Vail Resorts. Throughout the years, I then raced in high school where I led our team to the State Championship then coached the team for a year when I was a senior in college.
- Are you a beer snob? What's your favorite type of beer? What about your favorite beer overall?

  If it's in front of me, I'm going to drink it. *For me, beers fall into two categories—party beers and drinking beers*. Miller Lite is a party beer. Bell's Oberon is a drinking beer.
- What types of places are your favorite to eat? Hole in the wall? Ethnic food? Upscale? Trendy? Something else? How do you usually find these places?

  Pizza is life but I want to try everything, so I read a lot about restaurant openings then get my friends on board to come with me. Some are trendy, some are classics.

List at least three things that you really just enjoy.

An Americano on Friday morning (weekly coffee treat), new Nike sneakers, *football especially Michigan State*, the Denver Broncos, *being away from my phone*, *Red Rocks Amphitheater*, *short rib sandwiches*, ping pong, hot tubs, Spotify, beer, bike rides, *camping*, *working out a lot*, Under Armour, companionship, waffles, *making dumb bets*, books, classic/timeless looks like wayfarers. Could keep going but probably good for now.

- MSU football! How big of a fan are you? Do you watch games on TV? Do you ever go to games?

  I am a super fan. I rarely miss watching a game, I follow every social media account, and know what is going on with the team all the time. I usually make it to two to three games a year. Two usually in East Lansing then the bowl game. In the past two years, I have been to the Rose Bowl and Cotton Bowl. Michigan State won both games.

- And a Broncos' fan too. Ever go to games?

  Not much to root for in Detroit when I grew up in terms of pro football so I actually had adopted the Broncos before I moved to Denver. I remember this Monday Night Football game they were playing here, it was snowing, and I was hooked. I go to one to two Broncos games a year but they are almost too expensive to attend.

- How often do you camp? What's the longest trip you've ever been on? Do you ever go solo or always with friends?

  Three to four weekends a summer. Longest I have been on is a six-day backpacking trip through the Grand Tetons which was too fun. Never go alone, it's not safe if something happened to me! I'm usually a very careful Eagle Scout, but you never know what could happen. Proper prior preparation prevents piss poor performance!

- Tell me a cool/interesting/funny story about a time that you were camping.

  So when I was younger, I was a sleep walker. One night at Boy Scout camp, *I went on a sleep walking adventure and woke up from the sleep walk in the middle of the woods without shoes on wrapped in a sleeping bag with no idea where I was.* However, I was able to *locate the north star and orient myself* then find my way back to camp. Didn't know I would be using the skills I learned up there so quickly.

- Would you consider yourself generally outdoorsy? Anything that you won't do?

  For sure. *I love being outside as much as I can.* I don't like heights at all but other than that, I'm always down.

- What types of dumb bets do you make? Give me a few examples.

  Most are usually clothing oriented, so my buddy who is a Nebraska fan would have to wear Michigan State stuff. Others include the dollar challenge. The dollar challenge is based on figuring out how far someone will go to prove something since the money really isn't a motivation.

- What's the best dumb bet that you've ever lost, and what did you have to do?

  I got dollar challenged to wear a bathrobe to a bar. I love bathrobes and I am not afraid of attention, so I ate it up and got a few numbers. *Make sure whenever you wear a bathrobe to a bar it has pockets.*

In the last six months, what's the most interesting thing you've done or accomplished?

  I skied the back bowls at Vail, which had ten inches of powder, because I was able to get out of work.

Your Match

In a few sentences, describe your ideal match.

  She is *direct and confident*. She lets you know she *wants to be a part of your life* and doesn't always let you come to her, she asks you to do things too. She is mysterious and doesn't lay it all on the table right away but is very *caring and affectionate*. She's probably *going to have to be a little nuts to keep up with me and isn't along for the ride*. She doesn't take things too seriously but still has her own direction. She doesn't expect me to push but support her no matter what she is doing. *She randomly writes me notes on Post-Its and puts them on stuff. We like exploring together*. We randomly book tickets to cities and go there to eat and hang out. She has to be a *little spontaneous*. We both give the relationship 100 percent but we also have some things we like to do without the other person as our things but the other still knows all about what happens. *She would still get to see her friends a lot and I would get to see mine* but we wouldn't do the whole lame Harry Houdini act. She would also *randomly surprise me with baos. I love baos.*

Homework
Now, find at least two people who know you really, really well. Ask each to list, off of the top of his or her head, six things that you *love.*

Friend 1:
>A well-crafted Spotify or Soundcloud playlist including some nice jams and some high-quality remixes
>A long run at twilight in a long sleeve t when the temperature is in the mid-forties
>A banana that just turned yellow and some crunchy peanut butter
>*Frozen blueberries*
>Schmidt from *New Girl*
>*Any relatively mundane competitive event that gets taken a little bit too seriously by everyone involved*

Friend 2:
>Enthusiasm for adventure
>*Laughing till it hurts*
>*Chasing powder days & blue skies*
>Quality exotic/new cuisine
>*Lifting weights/Beastmode thighs*
>Beyonce lyrics

Friend 3:
>Michigan summers
>*Mildly embarrassing, head-nodding pop music*
>*Outdoor drinking games*
>*Dinner parties*
>Extreme team workouts
>*High-caliber hugs*